POSITIONAL HITTING

THE MODERN APPROACH
TO ANALYZING AND TRAINING
YOUR BASEBALL SWING

POSITIONAL HITTING

THE MODERN APPROACH
TO ANALYZING AND TRAINING
YOUR BASEBALL SWING

BY JAIME CEVALLOS

Mill City Press, Inc.
212 3ʳᵈ Avenue North, Suite 290
Minneapolis, MN 55401
612.455.2294
www.millcitypublishing.com

ISBN - 978-1-936107-91-9
ISBN - 1-936107-91-0
LCCN - 2010928504

Printed in the United States of America

DEDICATION

This book is dedicated to those who love the feeling of a perfect hit and dream of doing it more often, in front of more people.

For my wife, Suriati, for believing in me long before I believed in myself.

INTRODUCTION

*"Discovery consists of seeing what everybody has seen
and thinking what nobody has thought."*
-Albert von Szent-Gyorgyi

What is the one thing that sets apart the greatest hitters in baseball – Babe Ruth, Ted Williams, Albert Pujols – from the rest? I can tell you that it is not their strength, confidence, or hand/eye coordination, as many believe. We have all seen strong, confident, and coordinated kids quit baseball early on and pursue sports that encourage and celebrate these attributes, like basketball and football. What separates the great hitters from the average hitters is much less apparent, at least to the naked eye: the answer is their positions. More than anything else, the positions a hitter achieves through the baseball swing significantly increase or decrease his odds of success. So the questions that naturally follow are: what are the key positions and how does one train to achieve them? *Positional Hitting* answers these questions.

By the time you finish reading *Positional Hitting*, you will understand the baseball swing in such a way that, with the help of a camcorder, you will be your own best instructor going forward. *Positional Hitting* gets right to the heart of the matter - the biggest obstacles to hitting with high levels of power and consistency are very small changes in your swing positions. The once mystical art of hitting is actually a very explainable skill.

You will see that games are not decided by a few plays, but by the continuous battle for the hitter's positions – the *true* game within the game. The pitcher, by changing his delivery, and the movement, speed and/or location of his pitches, attempts to "pull" the hitter out of position, forcing him to make weak contact with the baseball or swing and miss entirely. Should the pitcher be effective and the hitter undisciplined in his positions, a swing that starts out as a home run instantly turns into a ground ball – a base hit into a strikeout.

This is the invisible game within the game that determines player's careers. This game has never before been discussed in such depth and detail as you will see in this book.

Positional Hitting will unveil this once invisible scrap for positioning between pitcher and hitter and show you how to use this knowledge to drastically improve your hitting in very little time. Baseball is truly a game of inches, not in the way the ball bounces, but in the positions achieved by the hitter through his swing.

MY STRUGGLE TO HIT

I was always self-motivated to become a better hitter, not one of those kids pushed by my parents. What started as an innocent hobby grew more intense with age. As I got older, hitting became an obsession. By the start of high school, I had already read numerous biographies of great hitters – like those of Pete Rose and Babe Ruth – in hopes of finding a secret to hitting somewhere in the pages. But they only showed me what type of person they were, and it was evident that a wide array of personalities can make a great hitter. Pete Rose, a slap hitter, was serious about winning and very aggressive on the field. Ruth, the opposite of Rose, was a power hitter with a laid back demeanor, often waving to the fans while rounding the bases after he hit a home run. I learned a lot about these great hitter's personalities but continued to struggle with my own hitting.

The summer before my sophomore year in high school, I worked at the local golf course for an entire summer so I could buy a wiffle ball pitching machine. I wore this thing out, using it in my backyard for hours every day. This didn't help my hitting either because, while I was seeing more pitches, my mechanics remained the same. I stuck with it, however, until it broke down two years later. I now realize that you can hit baseballs until your hands bleed, but without changing your swing positions, you are basically the same hitter.

I read all of the popular instructional books and followed their instruction precisely. They all seemed to advocate entirely different methods, which confused me. How could there be such a discrepancy in the methods of hitting coaches? To add to my confusion, no matter which method I tried, my hitting would not improve. The problem was that none of these books taught *key positions* - precise positions that, when achieved, would instantly make you a better hitter.

A perpetually bad hitter, I began to think, as I'm sure many players do, that hitting was a natural born skill that I just didn't have. I told myself, however, to not give up yet. In the meantime, I made myself a defensive specialist. I became one of those shortstops whose flashy play makes people forget about their poor hitting.

Despite the advice that my hitting and below average running speed were more suited for Division 3 baseball, I was determined to play Division 1. In 1996, a year after graduating from high school, I made the baseball team at Mount Saint Mary's University as a walk-on and quickly earned the starting shortstop position. While my defense remained solid, I finished my freshman season with a .197 batting average and just one extra base hit, an "excuse me," blooping pop-up that landed between the first baseman and right fielder that I legged out for a double. I would get two or three grounders per game on defense, my chance to show off flare on the field, but I had to face the facts - baseball just isn't fun if you aren't hitting. At the end of my freshman season, I vowed to look into the baseball swing on my own and see if I could figure something out that would finally turn me into a good hitter.

MY IMPROVEMENT

During the offseason after my freshman year, I spent a lot of time contemplating my own struggle to hit. It seemed I had tried everything. There was one aspect, however, that stood out. When playing shortstop during games, I could tell the good hitters from the average hitters by the look of their swings.

The bat path of good hitters remained on a flat plane for a long time through the hitting zone while the average hitters' swing plane shifted through the zone. If the hitter had a flat, continuous-plane swing, I could expect a lightning fast ground ball, so I would take six or seven steps back until I was in the outfield grass. If the hitter's swing-plane shifted, I moved in a little. This tactic helped me numerous times per game.

A good baseball swing is controlled by the bigger muscles in the legs. The arms work as a whip and the bat stays on one consistent plane through the swing.

In an ineffective baseball swing, the arms fire the bat outward prematurely. This can be seen from the fielder's perspective because the bat changes planes through the swing

Why couldn't I use this same knowledge, I thought, to improve my offense? It suddenly seemed obvious to me in the summer after my freshman season, that if I could recognize good hitters by the way their swing looked from the field, the secret to hitting must be in the positions a hitter achieves through the swing. I had no idea at the time that this minor revelation would start me down a path that would, a decade later, lead to working independently with Major League Baseball players on their swing mechanics.

At that time, all that mattered to me was that I had narrowed the secret to hitting to a single word: positions. I started cutting out pictures of great hitters in mid-swing from back issues of *Sports Illustrated*. I brought the pictures to the aerobics room at the University's athletic facility because one wall of the room was a huge mirror that would provide me with the visual feedback I needed. I would recreate the positions of the professionals in the pictures. Then I would move into the positions that I was achieving in games, going back and forth, from my positions to the professionals'. The difference was obvious.

The biggest difference was in the Impact position, the point of contact with the baseball. The Impact position that I achieved during games was much more "disconnected," my hands far from my body. A few years would pass before I learned the specific key angles that great players achieve at Impact. There in the aerobics room, I just felt that the professionals had a "tight" Impact position, their hands close to their body. Although not precise, it was still a valuable discovery. And this made sense to me. More of the player's body mass was being transferred to the ball if the hands remained closer to the body at Impact. Finally, I began to understand the baseball swing on my own terms.

When I attempted to turn this new Impact position into a movement and achieve it within a swing, it felt strange. My swing never felt this different before, so I knew that I was onto something. And I soon found that while the new swing felt strange at first, it became more comfortable as I practiced.

When hitting balls off of a tee with my new swing, I could see the ball coming off of the bat with much more speed than before. I was swinging effortlessly and hitting the ball with much more power. The true test, however, would be in how my new swing performed in games. That test came the following season - my sophomore year.

From the very beginning, there was an obvious difference. In the first two weeks of the season, I had a four-for-four-game and two home runs. Up to that point, I had never had a 4-4 game or hit even one home run *in my life*! The best way I can describe the feelings I had in those first two weeks is to compare it to what it would feel like if you just discovered you were Superman. I spent many hours as a little kid taking three steps and then jumping, hoping that I would start flying and everyone would cheer as I made my way to the clouds. That never happened, but I was sure in the clouds when I finally started to hit the baseball. To this day my motivation to teach the baseball swing comes from seeing others achieve this same feeling – pure happiness and excitement.

Adding to my feeling of euphoria was the fact that I was not working nearly as hard on my hitting as before. Prior to my revelation, I thought hitting was about hand/eye coordination, so I spent hours and hours hitting wiffle golf balls with a thin barreled training bat, hoping my hand/eye coordination would finally "come around." But now I was sure that hitting was about swing positions, so whether my practice lasted five minutes or forty-five minutes, all that mattered was keeping my new positions, my new swing, intact.

After games, I spent just ten minutes reinforcing my new swing in the comfort of my air-conditioned dorm room. That was the only practice I would need during the season. Aside from pregame, I practically quit taking batting practice. It just wasn't necessary. I was practicing less - a lot less - and was hitting far better than I ever had in my life. I ended that season with a .364 batting average, fourth in the league, and four home runs. I had raised my OPS by 501 points from my freshman year and earned the first team All-Conference award as a shortstop. I had done what no book, coach, or training aid could do for me – I had made *myself* into a good hitter. And I did it by changing a few positions through my swing. I had cracked open a door to a world that nobody else seemed to know exist – the door to Positional Hitting.

TRADITIONAL INSTRUCTION

Changing the positions you achieve through the swing can result in the quickest improvement in your power and consistency. If you don't realize this, your practice routine will look a lot like those of the typical team or player. Walk into the local hitting facility in your town and you will likely see coaches using ball-flight (the flight of the ball after contact) as their main source of feedback. It goes like this: the player hits live pitching and, depending on how the player hits the ball, the coach responds with either instruction or praise. When the player hits the ball poorly, the coach tells him that his mechanics were off. When the player connects and hits one well, the coach says, "See? You did it right on that one. Good job." The coach is looking like a genius, but the player is not getting better.

Ball-flight is a poor source of feedback for swing mechanics and yet I see instructors using it in their lessons time and time again. The skill of hitting is about percentages. You are not going to hit the ball perfectly with every swing, so the real challenge of hitting is to achieve swing positions that *increase your odds* of hitting the ball perfectly. Using ball-flight as feedback is unreliable because anyone can crush a pitch every once in a while, especially when the instructor is serving up "meatballs" at the same speed. It doesn't mean your swing was good; it just means the law of averages came around in your favor on that particular pitch. The difference between great hitters and average hitters is that great hitters crush pitches *more often*. The odds work in the great hitters' favor because they achieve better positions through the swing.

Never use ball-flight as a source of feedback. The most reliable source of feedback is video. Like I often tell my students, "video doesn't lie." The swing flaws you currently have, whether you hit a home run or strike out, will show up on video just the same.

The *books* on hitting have also come up well short of the mark, most citing principles and positions that have little or no correlation to great hitting. The inability of "hitting gurus" to base their principles on true *key* positions of the swing has left players thinking more, trying harder, but getting worse. The advantage therefore, has gone to the players who stay away from mechanical advice completely. The KISS principle – "Keep It Simple, Stupid" - has unfortunately reigned supreme. "Just use the swing that you were born with and be aggressive," they reason, "at least it's better than clogging your mind with mechanical jargon." But the KISS principle has only ruled because of a lack of quality instruction, not because it is better to avoid thinking about your mechanics.

In Charlie Lau's book, *The Art of Hitting .300 (Penguin Books - 1980)*, he lists his ten laws of hitting. Rule number six is an "aggressive move toward the pitcher when swinging." But how does one know when he has or has not made an aggressive move? What if the hitter *felt* aggressive? Is that enough? Can the hitter's move be *too* aggressive? There is no way to measure the rule and therefore it does not provide the hitter with a precise way of obtaining feedback and measuring his progress. The rule is too vague.

Rule number eight is "keeping your head down at the point of contact," but Babe Ruth and Ted Williams both lifted their heads through the swing. We're talking about the number one and two hitters of all time! Unless a hitting coach is churning out hitters that are better than Ruth and Williams, "keeping your head down at the point of contact" can't be a law. The problem with this law is that it lacks a direct, positive correlation to hitting with more power and consistency.

While Lau helped hitters and was a formidable hitting coach in his day, it's time for a new approach.

POSITIONAL HITTING – A NEW APPROACH

Positional Hitting is based on the fact that the main challenge of hitting is in modifying the swing positions to work in the hitter's favor as much as possible. This book challenges coaches and players to be more efficient in their practices by spending a majority of the time analyzing swings on video and training swing positions, rather than mindlessly hitting batting practice. Can you imagine a two-hour hitting practice session in which there is not one baseball thrown? That is the future of hitting.

Positional Hitting brings a systematic approach to improving your hitting so you always know where you stand with regard to your mechanics. The key positions will be the foundation of your analysis and training and there are three reasons why:

1. The key positions have a *direct positive correlation to more power and consistency.*

Each key position has a confluence of benefits, tremendously decreasing the pitcher's historically inherent advantage over the hitter. The key positions simultaneously...

- *...increase the force behind the bat as it travels through the hitting zone.*
- *...lengthen the **Area of Impact (AOI)**, the distance that the bat is square enough to the line of flight of the baseball through the hitting zone to transfer adequate force to the*

ball (in other words – how long the bat stays square through the zone).
- *...improve the player's timing of his swing.*
- *...improve the player's pitch selection.*

The confluence of benefits explains why every so often there is a hitter who hits with tremendous power and consistency year after year, and does so effortlessly. Players like this achieve a good number of the key positions within their swing.

The key positions you will see in this book are the most perfect form of that particular stage in the swing, giving you a glimpse into how the baseball swing will change in the next twenty years. The swings of players in the near future will be so much better that watching footage of today's hitters will remind us of a time when video analysis and swing positions were not taken as seriously.

The Positional Hitting method does not look to copy players from the past, but to improve upon their positions and allow hitting to evolve to a level that has yet to be seen. Babe Ruth got into great positions, but nobody is interested in seeing another Ruth. I believe *Positional Hitting* will be integral in producing the next hitter to bat over .400 and the first hitter to amass 80 home runs in a season in the Major Leagues. Feats like that are not accomplished by doing what has already been done with regard to swing mechanics.

2. The key positions are measured using precise angles as seen on video for accurate feedback.

Players often prefer to be vague when analyzing their swing. Criticism can be hard to take. "Your Angle D is at 100 degrees and to hit with power, you have to be above 120," sounds a lot harsher than "try to keep your head down a little more." However, the former is the language of Positional Hitting, and while it is more forthright, it provides the player with accurate feedback. If you truly want to improve, you must honestly assess your current swing mechanics. That means using video as your main source of feedback and being particular about your positions and angles as seen on video.

3. The key positions can be trained using drills that lead to immediate improvement.

Positional Training is quite unique. As one of my Major League students once said, "This is like swing yoga." There is no moving baseball in any of the drills. The training is inwardly focused and the purpose is to continuously improve your swing positions. As I said before, the main challenge of hitting is positional. The pitcher's two main goals are: 1) to throw strikes and 2) to pull you out of powerful and consistent swing positions. The best way to defend against this is to continuously hone more powerful and consistent swing positions in your training.

While Positional Training may be difficult at first, if you stick with it, you will reach a moment of clarity where the positions turn into a fluid movement. Improvement in your swing positions is not a consistent and gradual climb. Rather, it comes in sudden leaps – "aha moments" if you will. How quickly you improve depends on your willingness to change. If you are open to change, Positional Training can improve your hitting, literally, overnight.

CHAPTER CHALLENGE

Express Your Goals Openly. For the next month, write your goals (baseball related or not) on a piece of paper and post it where others will see. Although many people want to deny it, what you achieve in your life is a reflection of you. But don't let that put pressure on you. Enjoy it. People often don't want to be associated with any goals because they are afraid of what people will say if they fail. The road to achievement, however, is littered with failure. Don't fall into the trap of seeing a failure as anything but an opportunity to improve.

Failures are also opportunities to gain an edge on the competition. You have to assume that your competitors are confronted with roughly the same amount of failures and to roughly the same degree that you are. You also have to assume that many of these failures stop your competitors in their tracks and slow down their progress. Therefore, the less time you spend wallowing in your misery and the faster you get up and keep moving forward, the faster you will move ahead of the competition.

By posting your goals for others to see, you are forced to talk openly about your dreams. This will be good for you. It's not important what others say about them. The act of expressing your goals is more about putting yourself in the right mind-set than it is about what others say. When people inquire about your goals, talk openly about them. Don't be afraid to tell people how important your goals are to you. Remember that every failure is only an opportunity to learn; it is nothing to be embarrassed about. This mentality will keep the pressure from mounting and keep you moving quickly towards your goals.

CHAPTER ONE

MYTHS AND MISCONCEPTIONS

*"The fight is won or lost far away from witnesses – behind the lines, in the gym,
and out there on the road, long before I dance under those lights."*

– Muhammad Ali

After my turnaround season in college, I devoted the next ten years to studying the baseball swing. I moved to Charleston, South Carolina, where I worked in the golf industry and learned about the various swing analysis software and how golfers use video to improve their swings.

In 2001, I met with the manager of the local professional baseball team, the Charleston Riverdogs, to ask if he would be open to the idea of allowing me to film the players' at-bats from the dugout and making the video readily available to the players during games. The manager was Buddy Biancalana, a World Series champion for the Kansas City Royals. Buddy was suspicious when I told him I wanted to volunteer my time and that I didn't need to get paid. "People don't do things for free," he told me in his office. Despite his apprehension, Buddy agreed to let me film his hitters and every once in a while paid me fine-money (collected from players when they were late for meetings).

I learned a lot about the swing during my time filming Riverdogs hitters, but I learned even more about how hitters are instructed. Instruction at the professional level wasn't much different from what I had experienced as a player in high school or college. This surprised me.

Normally, the Riverdogs' hitting coach stood behind the batting screen during batting practice before games and gave players one or two swing thoughts to keep in mind. This was quite perplexing. The work on mechanics should have already been done, I thought, long before pregame batting practice. Besides, real and lasting change doesn't occur during batting practice. Real change only comes with conscious effort and focus on the swing mechanics, in front of a mirror or off of a tee.

I had thought that at the higher levels of baseball, coaches and players would get into the mechanics of the swing in more depth, but they didn't. Overall, the hitting coach for the Riverdogs focused more on the mental aspect of hitting than the mechanical, keeping the hitter's confidence up and his focus off of the bad at-bats. Again, this was confusing to me. I was certain by this time that the only way to get better was to look square in the face at bad swing habits. I understood that positive thinking will make the hitter *feel* better, but it was the bad at-bats that provided *opportunity*. If one was ignoring his shortcomings, he was ignoring the opportunity to improve.

The Riverdogs pitching coach, on the other hand, would get in-depth about mechanics. He would often ask me to film their "franchise" pitcher at the time, Matt White, who signed with Tampa Bay for $10.2 million. After games, the two would look at White's mechanics on my laptop and analyze the various positions he was achieving through his motion. "If you continue to release from this position," the coach would tell White, "you're going to have much less velocity and possibly get injured." During White's next few days off, he would work on changing the mechanics of his delivery. Why wasn't this same process, I wondered, employed for the hitters?

Over and over again throughout my years studying the baseball swing, hitting coaches would shy away from getting too technical about mechanics while pitching coaches would talk more openly about mechanics. It seems that hitting coaches avoid mechanical advice for fear that the player will start over-thinking at the plate.

Thinking about swing mechanics remains taboo in baseball. Players avoid it like the plague. But the problem has not been in thinking about mechanics. It's been in *how* hitters think about mechanics. The *Positional Hitting* approach makes it ok for you to delve into analysis of your swing by giving you a systematic approach to hitting. There is a cycle to training if it is done efficiently. Different actions should be performed at different times and not meshed together as they have been in the past. There are three categories of actions:

- **Know the Key Positions**
  You must know where you want to go if you ever want to get there. The key positions that you will learn in Chapter 2 are your ultimate destination. The first step is to know and understand the key positions of the swing.

- **Obtain Feedback**
  If you want to arrive at your goal, you must know where you are. Don't trust "feel" or "ball-flight" to tell you, either. Video should be your only master. The feedback of video is the most reliable indication of where you are with regard to your mechanics.

- **Training**
  You know where you are and where you want to go, now it's time to start moving. The final step is to make changes to your swing mechanics, keeping in mind the ultimate goal – the key positions.

The cycle of improvement

PITCHING IS WINNING THE BATTLE OVER HITTING

It's no wonder that a popular saying among baseball coaches and analysts is "Pitching wins Championships." Hitting can too, if it ever catches up.

Since the beginning of professional baseball, pitchers are steadily increasing their edge over hitters. The list of top ten hitters in adjusted OPS, the statistic that is said to be the best measure of a player's offensive worth, contains just one active player, Albert Pujols. Aside from Pujols and Barry Bonds, the rest of the players on the list played their entire careers before 1965!

The best way to measure a pitcher's worth is up for debate but in looking at the top ten pitchers in Adjusted ERA (ERA+), as I write this, there are four active pitchers on the list and five played *after* 1965.

1. Babe Ruth
2. Ted Williams
3. Barry Bonds*
4. Lou Gehrig
5. Roger Hornsby
6. Mickey Mantle
7. Dan Brouthers
8. Joe Jackson
9. **Albert Pujols**
10. Ty Cobb

The top ten hitters of all time ranked by career adjusted OPS. Players shown in bold are currently playing in the Major Leagues.

*Although I've included him, I do not consider Bonds' swing as a swing worthy of being on this list. His CSR, a measurement of his swing mechanics, averages around 340 to 370 which means he had a good swing but certainly not a swing that ranks among the top hitters of all time.

1. **Mariano Rivera**
2. **Pedro Martinez**
3. Lefty Grove
4. **Trevor Hoffman**
5. Walter Johnson
6. **Johan Santana**
7. Dan Quisenberry
8. Ed Walsh
9. Hoit Wilhelm
10. Joe Wood

The top ten pitchers in Adjusted ERA (The players shown in bold are currently playing in the Major Leagues.)

The power and consistency of hitters has dropped significantly since the early days of professional baseball. Arguably the best hitter of all time, Babe Ruth had an average of .373 with 46 home runs in 1931 and he was *fifth* in the MVP voting. In 1988, Kirk Gibson *won* the MVP award with a .290 average and 25 home runs.

The most obvious sign of the decline of hitting, however, is batting average. There hasn't been a .400 hitter since Ted Williams batted .406 in 1941. Prior to 1941, players had hit at least .400 twenty seven times. That's twenty eight times that players achieved a .400+ average in the first 65 five years of Major League Baseball and zero times in its last 67 years!

THE DECEPTION OF STEROIDS

Despite evidence that hitting has been on a steady decline in relation to pitching, the "Steroid Era" fooled many people. Before it was common knowledge that steroids ran rampant in Major League Baseball throughout the 1990s and early 2000s, numerous articles and books were written in attempt to explain the sudden surge in power. The question on everyone's mind: "How are these guys hitting so many home runs?" In *The Art of Hitting .400 (Addax – 2000)*, Charlie Lau's son, Charlie Lau Jr. writes, "Over the past ten years, there has been nothing short of a revolution in hitting." He went on to explain this revolution:

> "In one word: technique. It's clear to me that hitters have improved greatly in their approach and their technique. And that fact, more than anything, explains the rise in offensive production and runaway inflation of earned run averages."

However, with the overwhelming evidence of the Mitchell Report, it is now clear that the extraordinary statistics of many hitters during the 1990s and early 2000s were attributable to drug use and increased muscle mass, not to a sudden improvement in hitters' technique. An increase in muscle mass not only increases the hitter's bat speed through the zone, but also adds mass and therefore increases bat force, the overall force transferred to the ball at contact. Barry Bonds gained 40 pounds of muscle, allegedly from the use of steroids. The balls that Bonds formerly hit to the warning track would make it over the outfield wall for home runs thanks to the added muscle. Additionally, by having faster bat-speed, the hitter is able to wait longer on the pitch, giving him more time to assess the pitch's location before committing to swing. Steroids, despite the continuous debate as to how much they actually help, do in fact give hitters a tremendous advantage. It was cheating, plain and simple.

THE REASON PITCHING IS WINNING: MECHANICS

To get the most from his 5'9", 160 pound frame, Tim Lincecum, San Francisco's 2008 Cy Young Award winner, employs a unique pitching style. Fellow players refer to Lincecum as the "Freak," and a "mechanical marvel."

Lincecum starts his pitching motion fast, jumps toward the hitter, and keeps his shoulders closed until the very last moment before whipping his fastball upwards of 98 mph. The key to his motion is the tremendous flexibility and torque created between his hips and shoulders. At first, scouts were uncertain about his unconventional mechanics and suspected that his motion would lead to injuries. Lincecum was the 1408th pick in the 2003 Major League draft. Quickly proving his doubters wrong in his rookie season in 2007, he struck out 150 batters in 146 innings. Lincecum won back to back Cy Young awards in 2008 and 2009, striking out 526 batters in 452.1 innings during the two year stretch.

Lincecum's mechanics are different in that they are more efficient than any we have ever seen. The larger, stronger muscles in his legs and torso control his delivery, while his shoulders and the smaller muscles in his arms and hands work as a whip. His father and lifelong pitching coach, Chris Lincecum, used video analysis to teach Tim from an early age. He explains how his son gets so much from his small frame: "His mechanics are very efficient, extremely efficient. You don't see wasted energy." Not only does he throw harder than most pitchers, but he doesn't even ice his arm after his outings; because of his mechanics, he doesn't need to. (Verducci, Tom. "How Tiny Tim Became a Pitching Giant." Sports Illustrated July, 2008)

Lincecum's arrival should not surprise you. Since the beginning of baseball, circumstances have given pitchers the opportunity to improve their mechanics at a faster rate than hitters: Bullpens have given pitchers fertile ground on which to experiment and evolve; the four days between starts have given them adequate time to analyze their last performance; the pitching motion, unlike the swing, is slow and deliberate and can be analyzed quite well using the naked eye; and probably the biggest reason is that, out of necessity, pitchers oftentimes *have* to change their mechanics to avoid career ending injuries.

THE OLD MENTALITY IN HITTING

While pitchers have embraced mechanical change, the ethos among baseball coaches has been that great hitters are born, not made. In a 2002 article in Baseball Digest, writer Jerome Holtzman examined the curious role that hitting coaches play on Major League clubs. When he asked Al Lopez, who spent forty years in Major League Baseball as a player and manager for five different teams, if he knew of a hitting coach who has actually improved any hitters, Lopez replied with a chuckle, "No, I can't think of any." Holtzman also quotes Whitey Lockman, who spent 60 years around professional baseball and once famously remarked, "Only God can make a great hitter."

This mentality is understandable in players and coaches of yesteryear, as making changes to a player's swing mechanics without the aid of video analysis is an arduous task. Ted Williams wrote in his book *The Science of Hitting* (Fireside – 1986), that hitting is a matter of applying certain truths to a player's natural makeup. "If you've got a natural talent to work with," he writes, "you sure don't try to take anything away from him." This makes sense for a hitter at the time Williams wrote this in 1970 when there was a paucity of high-tech video equipment. Making a mechanical change to the swing was like blindly grabbing food in your fridge, mixing it together in a bowl and serving it for dinner. You're just *hoping* it turns out alright (and if it does, it doesn't mean you're a good cook). Without proper analysis, mechanical changes are nothing more than a guess.

As an example of the importance of continuously improving your swing mechanics regardless of how much success you are achieving, golfer Tiger Woods completely revamped his swing after winning all four golf majors in one year. This "overhaul" in his mechanics, adjusting just a few inches in the positioning of his arms and club through the swing, took over two years. Since then he has won six more majors, placing him among the best golfers in history.

After Tiger began to make changes to his swing, many writers criticized him for meddling with a swing that seemed to be working fine. But Tiger understands that you must *always* be improving your mechanics. Baseball players should learn from Tiger's example and embrace the tremendous benefits of mechanical change through video analysis.

There remains an underlying belief in baseball that you can't do anything to improve a hitter, only hurt him. Even when a player is struggling, nothing is done about it. For example, in response to what was happening to cause Derek Jeter's 0 for 32 slump in 2004, Yankees hitting coach at the time, Don Mattingly, told reporters, "He's swinging the bat all right. I think he's fine. We just need to get him hot" (Kepner, Tyler. "Jeter's Skid Is a Mystery With Few Clues." The New York Times 25 May, 2004).

And later that season, when Jeter began to come around, reporters again looked to Mattingly, "I don't really have an answer why he's doing well now. Just like I didn't have an answer for what was happening before. He's just doing his thing" (Caldwell, Dave. "For Jeter, Slump? What Slump?" The New York Times 28 June, 2004).

This mindset has to change. The trend of economic growth in professional baseball is such that a team can't afford to leave their hitting methodology to chance. While Mattingly was a great player, there can (and should) be more in-depth analysis done on the mechanics of hitters' swings. It's time for Major League Baseball teams to go outside of the pool of ex-Major League players when hiring coaches. The time will come when each hitter has his own swing instructor who helps him analyze and train his swing positions, hired by the team or the hitter himself.

ELEVEN MYTHS THAT HAVE HELD HITTERS BACK

In all of sports, there is no split-second motion as critical to an athlete's success as the moment a baseball player swings the bat. A good swing can mean the difference between hitting fourth in the lineup and hitting ninth. It can even mean the difference between earning millions of dollars per year and being a minor league journeyman. Despite its importance, traditional hitting instruction leaves those looking to improve their mechanics in the dark. There are eleven myths that are currently holding a majority of hitters back from hitting their best.

1. Power vs. Consistency Myth

Coaches often talk about power and consistency as if the player must sooner or later make a choice between one or the other. It's as if they don't even realize that players like Babe Ruth, Ted Williams, Albert Pujols, and Willie Mays even existed. They think only of players like Dave Kingman and Reggie Jackson who hit for power and not average, or players like Rod Carew and Wade Boggs who hit for average and not power. It's not only possible to have both, but it's easier to have both. That's why the greatest hitters, the ones who hit for power and consistency, had the sweetest swings and made it seem so easy.

I often encounter skepticism when I tell players that I can help them hit with more power and consistency in very little time just by changing the positions they achieve through the swing. Major League players, understandably, tend to be the most guarded. Their mentality is "if my swing got me this far, why change it?" But it isn't that their particular swing is flawed, it's that *all* swings are flawed. There are always opportunities for improvement in one's swing positions and that applies to even the best players in the world.

Once while working with a Major League player, he stopped me midway through our first session and said, "The coaches want me to be a situational hitter...to move guys around the bases. That's my job. If I start swinging for the fences, they're not going to like it." I told him that the positions that I teach add both power and consistency at the same time. The need to sacrifice consistency for power - a belief that coaches instill in kids from little league all the way to the Major Leagues - is a myth. "Don't try to hit home runs," they say, or "don't get too greedy; just make contact." But the fact remains that there aren't many seven figure contracts signed for slap hitters.

The good news is that you don't have to sacrifice power for consistency. In fact, the most consistent positions *are* the most powerful positions, and vice versa.

2. Hitting-is-Mental/Hitting-Is-All-About-Confidence Myth

There are two types of confidence, perceived confidence and real confidence, and both are a result—not a cause—of your performance.

Perceived confidence is the perception others have of you and is actually based 100% on your performance. If the player *succeeds*, onlookers point to his confidence as the cause. If the player fails, they point to his "lack of confidence."

Perceived confidence is the way people who aren't knowledgeable about the mechanics of hitting explain why a player succeeds or fails, but it is not a reason for success or failure at the plate. It is simply a perception *based* on the hitter's success or failure.

Real confidence is the way you feel about yourself with regard to a certain skill. In hitting, real confidence is the feeling of trust that your swing will yield results. This feeling is directly related to the quality of your swing positions and your subsequent success or failure. The more your swing positions increase your odds of success, the better your results and the more confidence you will have.

In either case, perceived or real, confidence is a result of performance, not a cause.

3. Hand/Eye Coordination Myth

Most of the hitting training aids are based on the belief that the key to improving your hitting is to improve your hand/eye coordination. The barrels have various shapes and sizes that "require more concentration and coordination from the player," so when he hits with a regular bat in games, it seems easier. But it doesn't work like that.

Most of the hand/eye coordination that it takes to hit a baseball is fully developed by the time you reach little league. From that point forward, hitting becomes a challenge of mechanics. If you have bad swing mechanics, all of the hand/eye coordination in the world won't help your hitting.

People who adhere to the hand/eye coordination myth also tend to believe that as long as your swing is repeatable and you learn to work with it, you can hit well. But that is not true. Your swing is *always* repeated. Your mechanics do not change from swing to swing (unless you are making a conscious effort to change them). You can see this by filming your swings off of a tee. Film ten consecutive swings off of a tee and stop the video at Impact, the point of contact with the baseball. All of your Impact positions will look identical. Swing mechanics don't change from swing to swing. If you have bad swing mechanics, you can try to work with them, but there will be a very limited potential for improvement.

4. Quick Hands Myth

Baseball coaches and analysts often talk about the importance of "quick hands" for hitting. But every great hitter has had very loose hands through the swing. Their "hand quickness" depends entirely on the speed of their body rotation. Therefore, it's the speed of their body rotation that is important.

The Quick Hands Myth exists because people tend to see what is most apparent and it's more natural to see the hands snap the bat through the zone than to see the legs straighten and the hips and shoulders rotate. However, it is the motion of these bigger muscles that guide the hands of every great hitter.

5. Game Mentality vs. Practice Mentality

I was invited recently to take a look at the swing of player, Josh, who was struggling at the plate playing for his summer-league team. Josh was getting nervous about entering his first year of college in the fall. He wanted to impress his new college coach from the beginning and he knew that the way he had been hitting that summer was not going to cut it in college.

I filmed four of Josh's at-bats during the first game of a doubleheader. After the game, I talked briefly with Josh. He told me what he thought he may be doing wrong mechanically. I could tell he wanted to know my thoughts on his swing and so I told him, "Josh, don't think about your mechanics right now. I have recorded every pitch thrown to you in four at bats. Whatever you are doing wrong, we will figure it all out later. For now, just focus on the baseball coming toward the plate. That's all."

We met the next day to go over his swing on video. We sat on the couch looking up at his positions on the flat screen. I pointed out the various opportunities for improvement in his mechanics and he was on the same page. Once he had a good understanding of where he was mechanically, I showed him what drills would be best for him to work on going forward. Josh ended up with the most home runs on the team in his first collegiate fall season and the highest batting average among the freshmen.

We had accomplished our goal: he was a shoe-in to be a starter in the spring. But I was most pleased about what Josh would tell me after the fall season: "Jaime, I just don't get mad after at-bats like I used to. It used to eat me up during the game when I made an out and it would affect my performance. But now I just tell myself, 'I'll look at the film and figure it out later.' Not only am I much better than I used to be, but my mind is freer during games as well. I can just play and have fun."

Josh learned that being analytical during games is counterproductive. It isn't making the out that "eats you up" during games; it's not knowing what *caused* it. Josh learned that during the game is not the time to try to figure that out. By filming his game at-bats, Josh achieved the peace of mind that everything would be figured out later. Always separate your game mentality from your practice mentality. The rule is: if the baseball is moving, don't think about your mechanics.

6. Extension Myth

I often hear coaches and analysts talk about the importance of "extension" at contact. Their thinking is that the player should extend his back arm toward the pitcher through the swing. The opposite is actually true. In a good swing, the back arm will not extend until well after contact with the ball. The best hitters keep their back arm bent deeper into the swing, letting the rotation of their body provide the power, not the extension of their back arm.

7. Rotational vs. Linear Hitting Myth

A debate continues among coaches about whether the swing is rotational or linear. Nowadays, it seems, hitting coaches stand on one side or the other. A good swing, however, is *three* things: it's linear, rotational, and it's also vertical (up and down).

As you will see, in order to properly build energy from the ground up in the stride portion of the swing, you must learn to move your lower body in the proper sequence. This is covered in the Fall and Cushion portion of The Key Positions section of this book.

8. Forearm Myth

Recently a coach told me that he takes his players to the university's pool once a week so they can swing a bat underwater to improve their hitting. I immediately felt sorry for his entire team. Underwater swinging will make you *feel* like you are really dedicated to improving your hitting (and will even get you a few strange looks) but actually does nothing. I know from experience. I spent many hours before my first season in college swinging a bat underwater and batted .197 the following season.

Underwater swinging is ineffective because it works only forearm and hand muscles, and although coaches often talk about wrist and forearm strength being important for hitting, it's just not true. Great hitters hit the ball with wrist snap, not wrist strength. As long as the back arm stays quiet, the rotation of your body should *whip* the bat through the hitting zone. This is done by keeping your wrists and forearms loose through the swing. The only strength required in your wrists and forearms is enough to keep your grip on the bat.

9. Stay-Inside-the-Ball Myth

The "stay inside the ball" approach that many instructors advocate is a close relative of the "drive the ball the other way," "knob-to-ball," or "throw the hands" approach to hitting. This is the prevalent hitting method of our day, but it comes with many flaws. Mike Epstein, who subscribes to the "stay-inside-the-ball-approach," writes in his book *Mike Epstein On Hitting* (Coaches Choice – 2003) that the hands should "fire straight forward to extend 'through' the ball." He goes on to say that staying inside the ball "maximizes bat quickness and bat velocity, supports the hands at extension, and gives us more 'time' to look pitches over!"

This reasoning is wrong because as your hands fire outward toward the ball, the barrel of the bat doesn't pick up more velocity, rather it slows the barrel down and keeps it from entering the hitting zone for far too long. Not only does this decrease your bat speed, it also decreases your bat mass, the amount of weight behind the hit, because when the bat is finally square to the ball, the hands are far from the body (your center of mass). The farther the hands are from the body at contact, the less mass transferred to the ball.

In a stay-inside-the-ball swing, the AOI is short (as indicated by the vertical lines), less force is transferred to the ball, and the hitter must make his decision to swing too early.

In a good swing, you will create a long AOI (as indicated by the vertical lines), transfer maximum force to the ball, and be able to wait as long as possible before swinging because contact is made deeper in the zone.

Staying inside the ball also decreases your consistency because it shortens the Area of Impact (AOI), the distance that the bat is square to the ball through the hitting zone. Keeping your back arm quiet through the swing allows the barrel to whip into the hitting zone early and stay there longer, creating a long AOI and increasing your odds of making contact.

Lastly, staying inside the ball gives you less time, not more time, to "look pitches over" because contact is made farther out toward the pitcher when you fire your hands toward the ball. In a Positional swing, you will let the barrel enter the hitting zone early so that contact can be made "deeper" in the zone, giving you more time to assess pitch location.

10. Stay Back Myth

Keeping too much weight on the back leg is one of the biggest problems that I see with today's hitters. Those who advocate "staying back" think that if the player keeps his weight back, he can't be fooled on the pitch because he never has to commit - he can just quickly throw his arms out and make contact.

Major League Hitting Coach Rudy Jaramillo teaches hitters to keep their weight back through the stride. The staying-back approach that he advocates hurts hitters' performance because it shortens the player's AOI and decreases the force behind the bat as it moves through the zone.

Players who adhere to the "stay back" myth will often wave at pitches with just their upper bodies and arms. There is very little power and consistency behind a "stay back" swing and the mindset of those that stick with it is to just try to connect the bat to the ball, not to hit the ball with power. The coaches who teach this method fail to realize that by shifting his weight to the front side in the stride, as long as he keeps his shoulders closed, the hitter has not fully committed to the pitch; he has simply positioned himself to build his energy from the ground up, a more powerful and consistent way to swing. With training, he can learn to delay his forward swing, even though he has shifted his weight to the front leg. This is explained later when I talk about the Cushion and Secondary Cushion positions.

11. Keep-Your-Head-Down-At-The-Point-of-Contact Myth

The Keep-Your-Head-Down-At-The-Point-of-Contact Myth is the second cousin of the Hand/Eye Coordination Myth because those who believe that hand/eye coordination is the key to hitting also tend to believe in the importance of keeping your head down and eyes at the point of contact after contact has been made. Studies have shown, however, that hitters don't see the ball for the last ten feet before it reaches home plate anyway, so keeping your eyes on the point of contact is just for show. Technically, you could close your eyes at the start of your swing and it wouldn't make any difference.

Coaches may also believe that pulling your head is bad because they think that the player should extend his arms down the line (see Extension Myth and Stay-Inside-the-Ball-Myth above). The thinking is that if you extend your arms down the line (toward the pitcher), the bat will stay in the hitting zone longer. While the bat may be in the hitting zone longer, it is not square to the ball for nearly as long, and if the bat is in the zone but not square, what good is it doing?

VIDEO IS THE FUTURE
– THE "MICROMECHANICS" OF SPORTS

Athletes in recent years have been searching for an edge in the wrong places. They are working longer and harder to improve their strength and speed, and while you certainly have to work hard in these areas, if you work too hard, you reach a point of diminishing returns and even risk burn-out. Despite little opportunity for an edge in strength and speed, athletes continue to focus in this area. Feeling like there is no other way, many athletes have even resorted to taking steroids to gain an advantage. All the while, they are missing the next wave of opportunity, the undiscovered "gold mine" in sports – the frame by frame positions as seen on video.

The analysis of the detailed, frame-by-frame positions that athletes achieve through their motions, the "micromechanics," will mark the future of athletic advancement. Through video analysis, one second movements will be "stretched out," seen more clearly, analyzed more closely, and made more perfect. In the near future, the gurus who have discovered key positions within a sport will be sought after just as much as the top ten draft-picks. After all, one superstar remains just one superstar, but one great "micromechanical" guru can make a team of superstars.

That is not to say that video analysis has not been done before. Football and basketball coaches, in particular, have used video to improve their team's performance for years. However, traditionally it has been used on a more "macro" level – analyzing the positions of players in relation to other players, not the positions of body parts in relation to other body parts.

Full-scale incorporation of video in sports is comparable to the meshing of the internet into society. The internet was clearly valuable at first, but nobody knew for sure how it could best serve the public. It turns out, many years later, that the internet is only moderately good for grocery shopping but works very well for social networking. Similarly, video analysis works well on a "macro" level, but its real value is in analyzing the "micromechanics" – the split-second movements that make or break an athlete's career.

CHAPTER CHALLENGE

Brush Your Teeth With The Opposite Hand. For the next month (at least twice a day), brush your teeth with the opposite hand and don't cheat even once.

Positional Hitting theory is based on achieving success by changing your movements. This takes inward focus. The parts of your brain that direct this type of learning are your motor cortex and cerebellum. The coordination between these two parts of your brain is something that can be practiced and improved, making you more "in control" of your movements when training and changing your swing positions.

Brushing with the opposite hand will be difficult at first, but there will be a day when the brushing motion feels much more fluid. It will just click and you will be almost as good as you are with your regular hand.

The same thing will happen when you work on your swing positions. Many players quit trying to change their positions because it's uncomfortable at first. But if you stick with it, as you will with brushing your teeth, there is a moment where the new movement clicks. That's when you have your new swing. Your quest for a more perfect baseball swing will be marked by these "click" moments. With each "click" you achieve higher and higher levels of hitting (or brushing).

CHAPTER TWO

THE KEY POSITIONS
OF THE BASEBALL SWING

"Measure what is measurable, and make measurable what is not so."
– Galileo

THE SECRET TO HITTING LIES IN YOUR POSITIONS

Many theories on hitting have arisen through the years. When Ted Williams became the first person in the modern area to hit over .400 in a season, it was rumored that he could see the seams of the baseball as it came towards him. This led people to believe that great hitters have exceptional eyesight. Then, when Mickey Mantle, a strong country boy from Oklahoma, arrived and hit moon-shots high over the outfield wall of Yankee Stadium, people thought thick and powerful forearms were the key to hitting. Tony Gwynn, the only recent player to be in the top 20 in lifetime batting average, was said to work for hours off of a tee before and after the games, which made people speculate that simply spending time hitting off of a tee could be the answer. To this day, most theories on hitting have been of little help to the hitters themselves. Sure, they've led to some improvement in hitters through the years, but not drastic and immediate improvement that is possible by changing your swing positions.

The real secret to hitting is in continuously improving the positions that you achieve through the swing as seen on video. For those who attain the key positions, hitting is effortless and fun. For those who don't, hitting will always be a struggle.

The seven key positions of the swing are Fall, Cushion, Slot, Impact, Delivery, Finish and Guard. The Fall, Cushion, and Guard positions occur in the stride portion of the swing. The Slot, Impact, Delivery and Finish positions occur after the stride, in the forward swing. Within the five key positions there are five key angles. The key angles point to particular positions of your body and bat that provide the most detailed feedback so you can analyze your own swing with precision. They are Angle S, Angle L, Angle W, Angle E, and Angle D. You will learn about them as we go through the key positions.

THE CONFLUENCE OF BENEFITS OF THE KEY POSITIONS

As I mentioned earlier, a good baseball swing with the right key positions has a confluence of benefits that exponentially increase a batter's power and consistency. The four benefits of the key positions are:

1. Increased Force

Sir Isaac Newton's second law of motion says that *force = mass x acceleration, or F = ma.* To maximize the amount of force applied to the baseball, the hitter must increase both the acceleration (speed) of the bat and the mass behind the bat as it travels through the hitting zone. The importance of bat speed is well known, and the key positions will add a significant amount of speed to your swing. But rarely, if ever, do coaches talk about bat mass. By positioning the arms correctly through the swing, more body mass is transferred through the arms, into the bat, and ultimately to the ball.

2. Longer Area of Impact (AOI)

Area of Impact is the distance through the hitting zone that the bat is square enough to hit a fair ball. By increasing your AOI, you greatly enhance the likelihood of making solid contact with the baseball. In other words, you increase your consistency. Have you ever felt like you had a great pitch to hit, took your best swing, but hit the ball weakly for an out? It's not your hand/eye coordination that's to blame; it's your AOI.

3. Better Timing Control

You can have adequate force behind the bat and a long AOI, but if you don't swing the bat at the right time, you won't make contact very often. Increasing your swing force and AOI has to do with *how* you swing; having better timing control has to do with *when* you swing. Your swing positions - in particular, positioning your bigger muscles to control the swing - will improve your timing control. The Secondary Cushion position will be the key to controlling your swing timing.

4. Improved Pitch Selection

Your pitch selection will naturally improve when you improve your key angles and positions. There are two reasons for this:

Wait longer before swinging

One of the keys to great hitting is to be able to wait as long as possible before swinging. If you can wait longer, you will have more time to assess the pitch location. There are two ways to increase the length of time that you can wait before swinging.

The first way is to shorten the time it takes you from the beginning of the swing to the point of contact - in other words, to swing as fast as possible. As you will see, a fast swing must start in a good "ready" position. This will be the Cushion position. If you don't start your swing in a good position, you will be slower through the swing and will have to make your decision to swing early, causing you to swing at bad pitches.

The second way to wait as long as possible before swinging is to move your point of contact farther away from the pitcher (closer to the catcher). Coaches often refer to this as "letting the ball get deep," but what they don't realize is that players can only let the ball get as "deep" as their swing mechanics will allow. In a poor swing, the player makes contact with the baseball far out in front of the plate, forcing him to start his swing earlier. In a Positional swing, you will make contact with the baseball deeper in the zone, closer to the catcher.

In a bad swing, contact is made farther out in front, giving the hitter less time to assess the pitch location.

In a Positional swing, contact is made deeper, giving the hitter more time to assess the pitch location.

Swing restriction = better pitch selection

A player's pitch selection is relative to how many different pitch locations he can reach. A good swing is a tight swing, and hitters with tight swings tend to have better pitch selection because they can't reach pitches that are too far outside.

In a good swing, the back arm doesn't straighten until after contact is made, producing a tight/restricted swing through the hitting zone. This restricts your bat-reach and your ability to hit outside pitches. By restricting your bat-reach, your pitch selection will naturally improve as you will begin to understand that you simply cannot reach pitches outside of the strike zone.

FILMING YOUR SWING

Once you familiarize yourself with the key positions, recording your swing will show you where the opportunities are. Every failure at the plate can and should be translated into the breakdown in positions that resulted. If you were "out in front" or "tried to do too much," it's not enough to leave it at that. Identifying the breakdown in your positions on video transforms your faults into a "workable format." You can work on changing your positions, but you can't realistically work on not being "out in front" or not "trying to do too much."

When my students call to tell me about their current struggles at the plate, I want them to talk only in terms of the positions that they see on video. Oftentimes, the conversation ends right there because they haven't watched film yet. They want to talk about what they are *feeling*, but feel is not real. I tell them to look at their swing on video and call me when they can talk about the specific positions and angles they see.

Recording your own swing will be an integral part of your training. The positions of every swing tell a story about what happens, not just with that particular swing or at-bat, but your tendencies in *all* at-bats. Swing faults don't change from swing to swing. By seeing just one swing on video, I can tell exactly what kind of hitter I'm dealing with. Quite often I can guess, within a few digits, a player's typical home run and batting average production in a season.

TWO TYPES OF VIDEO FEEDBACK

There are two ways of filming and analyzing your swing. They are Perfection Filming and Feedback Filming.

1. Perfection Filming

In Perfection Filming, you will film swings made at a stationary (non-moving) baseball, for example off of a tee, and you will film and analyze in the same session. In other words, you will film your swing and go to the video to check your positions, make some adjustments through drills or mirror work, and then film again. With each swing, you look to improve your positions.

The goal in Perfection Filming is to make your positions as perfect as possible. Because the baseball is stationary, you can focus completely on your mechanics.

2. Feedback Filming

In Feedback Filming, the baseball is moving, you are in a game mentality, and your swing analysis will take place at a later time. Feedback Filming can be obtained during games, batting practice, or even soft toss. Your focus is off of mechanics and on just hitting the ball hard.

The purpose of Feedback Filming is to see prevalent errors in your swing during games. It's more like grading a test as opposed to Perfection Filming, where you are making changes on the fly. Feedback Filming gives meaning and purpose to your poor at-bats. You come to learn that bad days at the plate are actually opportunities.

TIPS FOR FILMING YOUR SWING

- Put the shutter speed as high as you can. This will ensure that the bat is not blurry through the swing, so angles can be drawn with precision. One over one thousand (or faster) is a good shutter speed. You can also switch your camcorder to "sports mode" if it has one (simple way to increase the shutter speed). Increasing the shutter speed will make the picture darker so it is best to film outside, on sunny days.
- Film your swings from the front angle.
- Place the camcorder at shoulder level when filming and ensure that the hitter's entire body and the bat are in the picture through the swing.
- If you have a computer with swing analysis software installed, analysis becomes much easier because you will be able to draw the necessary lines and angles over your positions.
- Always film swings in which you are making contact with a baseball because the swing you take when you don't have to square the bat to the ball is different from when you do. Players will tell me, "I don't get it - my on-deck swings feel so good and then I get up to the plate and I can't reproduce it." My answer is that your swings on deck feel good because there is no need to square the bat to a ball.

The "front angle" vantage point – the best direction from which to film your swing

THE CLS GRIP

The grip is a very important component to hitting with power and consistency. It is the one connection you have with your weapon - the bat. The amount of energy you transfer from your body to the bat and from the bat to the ball is greatly affected by your grip. Your grip should have three important characteristics. It should be consistent, loose, and small. Together, these characteristics create the acronym "CLS."

Consistent

A consistent grip means getting the maximum amount of hand surface touching the bat to begin the swing, and keeping it that way from start to finish. If any part of your hand comes off the bat through the swing, called "air bubbles," you are losing grip consistency.

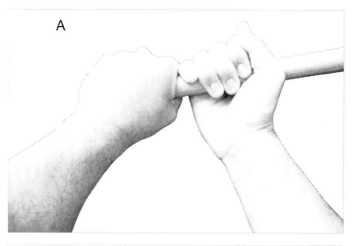

A

B

In an inconsistent grip (A), the hands fight each other, the bottom of the palm of the top hand coming off of the bat through the swing. In a good swing, the hands stay consistent (B). Practice feeling the grip stay consistent through the entire swing.

Loose

Keep the muscles in your hands and forearms loose, not just at the beginning and end, but throughout the entire swing. This allows your hands to whip the bat through the hitting zone with optimal speed and a long AOI.

Small

Push your hands close together so they work as one unit. The smaller the fulcrum is, the greater the speed that can be generated.

THE FALL POSITION

The Fall position occurs at the very beginning of the stride. *When analyzing your swing, the Fall is measured when the hitter starts his forward move in the stride.* The main purpose of the stride sequence is to "pull" energy from the Earth in the form of gravity to later turn it into rotational energy during the forward swing. Sounds really complex, but it's actually quite easy to understand.

Think of the stride like this: If I asked you to jump as high as you can from a standing position, your first move would be down before jumping up. By dropping down, you are momentarily relaxing your body so that gravity can briefly "take over." After falling momentarily, you would then push against this energy created by gravity in your upward jump. In this way, you have used gravity to create more force in your jump. This same type of sequence is seen in a good baseball swing. The Fall position, like the jump, is a momentary falling forward and down, in order to generate force later in the swing.

In addition to the forward and down motion that occurs in the stride, there is also a rotational aspect. As you begin the stride and achieve the Fall position, rotate your hips and shoulders away from the pitcher.

LET GO AND LET GRAVITY

It's important to understand that gravity works in its own time. Achieving a good Fall position will set you up to naturally fall forward. Falling is also the way your body generates movement when walking. Try it now: when you begin walking from a standing position, to make a step, your first move is to fall forward, followed by catching yourself with an extended leg. You can't force this fall forward, it happens in its own time.

For the player who employs the "toe-tap" stride, striding without shifting his weight, the Fall position will feel foreign at first. Players use the "toe-tap" because they believe it helps them time their swing. They think that if they never stride forward, they never actually commit to the pitch and therefore won't be fooled as often on off-speed pitches. The problem is that these players end up with a very defensive approach at the plate, often just swinging with the arms without any force from the lower body. There is a way, however, to fully commit to the pitch (shift your weight) and still control your swing timing. We'll discuss how you can control the timing of your swing when we talk about the next position, The Cushion.

Vladimir Guerrero is a player who gets into a great Fall position to begin his stride. Next time you get to see him hit, watch how he gets taller in the Fall and begins to wind himself up before falling forward and down in the stride.

"TF TRIPLE S" – THE MAGIC LOWER BODY MOVE

The lower body is the "engine" of the swing. While you will gently guide the shoulders and smaller muscles through the swing, for the most part, they behave passively, like a whip. Only the legs should be flexed and powerful when you swing. Correct lower body movement is referred to as "TF Triple S," which stands for Tall, Fall, Squat, Spin and Straighten. The first three happen in order and "Spin and Straighten" happens simultaneously.

The "TF Triple S" is the magic move of the lower body in order to build energy efficiently from the ground up.

STAY TALL IN THE FALL

Without a good Fall position, you are less likely to achieve any of the key positions that follow. When I see a player who gets taller to begin his stride, it tells me that he has a good understanding of how to begin the swing to build power slowly with the lower body. He understands the proper order of events to create a powerful swing. By getting taller as he shifts his weight back, he has farther to fall and more energy is built up for that split second when he spins and straightens to swing.

To ensure a good Fall position, think of keeping your back leg rigid as you shift your weight back. I often see players bend their back knee, getting lower at this stage of the swing. They are mixing up the proper order of events. It's like a basketball player shooting the ball and *then* jumping. It's not that you should never tense your legs and hips in the swing, it just happens later, after the stride, as you spin and straighten in the forward swing.

You have to train the beginning of your stride to the point that, even in the midst of game-time pressure, you will remain relaxed and allow gravity to take over to begin the swing. Proper repetition will be the key.

WIND THE HIPS IN THE FALL

Always remember that the legs and hips control the swing. The amount that you turn your hips away from the pitcher in the Fall will determine, in large part, your level of power and consistency.

You will notice that by turning your hips away from the pitcher in the Fall, when you land in your stride, you will momentarily have more torque between your hips and shoulders. Your hips, in essence, will whip your shoulders through the forward swing. This is what you want.

Your hips should be at their maximum turn away from the pitcher in the Fall. The hips will then turn back towards the pitcher as you land (again, leaving your shoulders behind momentarily). When trying to feel this in the beginning, it may help to turn your front heel toward the pitcher in the Fall and then when you land, have your front foot and front knee pointing toward the second baseman (shortstop for lefties). This will help you feel the proper motion of the hips through the stride.

SHIFT BACK OR GLIDE

In achieving the Fall position, you can either shift your weight back or start with your feet rather close together in your stance and glide directly into the Fall (Babe Ruth-style). Either way is fine, as long as you achieve a good Fall position prior to falling forward.

THE CUSHION AND SECONDARY CUSHION POSITIONS

The Cushion is the position from which you swing or take the pitch. *It is measured when your front heel lands after falling forward in your stride.* The next time you watch a baseball game, notice each player's Cushion position. Does the player lose the torque between his hips and shoulders, causing him to have to decide to swing too early? Does he put too much weight on his toes in the Cushion, resulting in "fishing" for outside pitches? Does he keep most of his weight on his back foot instead of his front, causing him to swing with just his arms? Failures at the plate can always be attributed to poor hitting positions and often the problem lies within the Cushion position, before the player even starts the forward swing.

After the Fall position, you will fall forward onto a bent front knee and land in the Cushion, with at least 60% of your weight on your front foot. A good Cushion sets you up to hit with power and consistency by positioning the bigger, stronger muscles in your legs and torso to control the swing. In the Cushion, you should be coiled and ready to release the torque between your hips and shoulders in the forward swing.

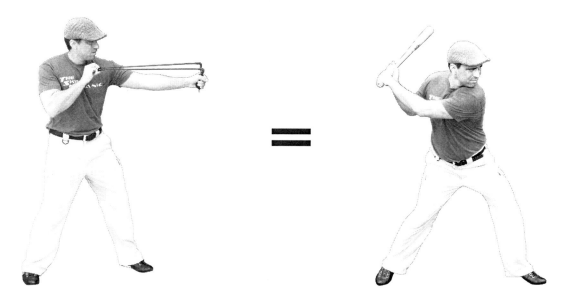

The Cushion position is similar to a slingshot pulled all the way back. There is only forward movement from here.

All movement from the Cushion is forward, so you can be quick and timely in your swing. If you were to compare the baseball swing to shooting a slingshot, the Cushion position is similar to the instant just before releasing the slingshot, when the band is stretched as far as it can go.

SHOULDERS CLOSED/HIPS OPEN

In the Cushion, the shoulders should be closed and the hips should be slightly open. To feel this, point your front shoulder towards first base for righties (third base for lefties) and point the front knee and front foot towards the second baseman (the shortstop for lefties). This positioning ensures that torque has been created between the shoulders and hips. As you straighten your front knee and rotate your hips to initiate the forward swing, you will release this torque, creating power through the hitting zone.

If you draw a line through your shoulders and cross it with a horizontal line across your hips in the Cushion position, you have Angle S. Angle S should be no less than 20 degrees. Twenty five degrees is very good and thirty degrees is excellent. Ken Griffey Jr. gets into a good Cushion position, with regular Angle S measurements of 25 to 30 degrees.

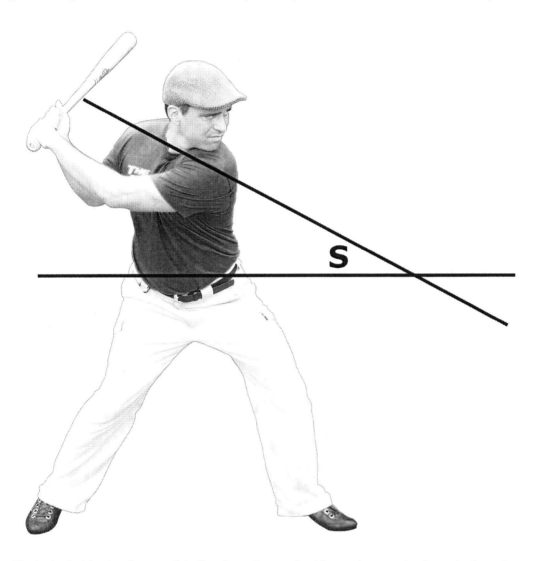

Obtain Angle S by drawing a straight line through your shoulders and connecting it to a horizontal line through your hips.

Your hips should be slightly open in the Cushion. If you land in the Cushion with the hips closed, when you decide to swing, your hips and shoulders will fire open simultaneously. When this happens you haven't created torque between your hips and shoulders and your swing will be slower and less powerful.

With the hips closed in the Cushion position, the hitter loses power and control of his swing

THE SECONDARY CUSHION – THE KEY TO TIMING

Every hitter has two positions from which he makes his decision to swing, depending on whether the pitch is a fastball or off-speed. Most hitters are unaware of these two points within their swing and they make hitting even more difficult by making their decision to swing from two very bad positions.

The first faulty position from which players decide to swing at the pitch is when their heel is up and their weight is back. From here, the player must decide to swing much earlier than necessary; the front heel must land and his weight shift before beginning his forward rotation. It takes too much time to get to Impact from here and the player will have to make his decision to swing way too early.

This is the first point from which most hitters mistakenly make their decision to swing. It takes too long to swing from here as the front heel has to land and the player's weight has to shift before he can swing.

This is the second point from which hitters mistakenly make their decision to swing. The hitter has no way to swing with force from here as the hips and shoulders are aligned and have lost their torque. This is when you see them wave weakly at a pitch with just their arms.

The second faulty position from which players decide to swing is when their weight has shifted to the front foot but the torque between the shoulders and hips has dissipated. In other words, their shoulders and hips are aligned. The "engine" of the swing, the bigger muscles, has broken down and the player can only extend his arms to swing the bat. If you see a player wave weakly at an off-speed pitch with just his arms, it may be caused by this.

The two best positions from which to make your decision to swing are the Cushion and the Secondary Cushion positions. Both positions will set you up for the quickest possible swing and offer the shortest amount of time between a decision to swing and contact with the baseball. This will naturally improve your pitch selection because, with a quick swing, you will have more time to assess the pitch location.

Setting your large muscles up to control the swing not only improves your swing speed and timing, it also produces optimal power and consistency through the swing itself. By whipping the arms and hands with the rotation of your hips and shoulders, you are almost guaranteed a consistent and powerful swing.

The Secondary Cushion position occurs when you land in your Cushion a little early and have to wait on the pitch. It is achieved by gradually increasing the weight on your front leg, increasing the bend in your front knee, and keeping the torque between your hips and shoulders intact.

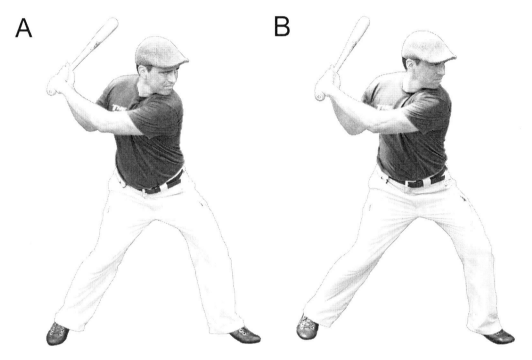

The Cushion (A) and Secondary Cushion (B) are the two best positions from which to swing. In the Secondary Cushion, the hitter has gradually increased the amont of weight on his front leg and the bend in his front knee.

The Secondary Cushion accomplishes a couple of things. First, it maintains movement and fluidity in your swing. If you stop moving altogether, it will be hard to start again. Second, the Secondary Cushion creates "reserve energy." With the forward momentum of the stride dissipating as you wait on the pitch, the additional bend in your front knee gives you a "backup energy supply." From the Secondary Cushion, you will straighten the front knee with great speed, drawing a majority of the power from your front leg. It's a slightly different feeling than a swing made on a well timed pitch, from the regular Cushion.

From your regular Cushion, the front-knee-snap will provide *some* of the power, but a majority of the power will come from your forward momentum. It will take some time to learn to generate power from these two different positions. Again, proper training will be the key in making both the Cushion and Secondary Cushion feel natural.

LAND IN A STRAIGHT LINE

Usually players want to stride toward the plate, especially righties because they are subconsciously getting a head start to first base. Pitchers love to see a hitter striding in toward the plate because he will tend to chase pitches that are too far outside and won't be able to handle pitches on the inside corner; this is just the combination the pitcher is looking for.

One of my students was intentionally striding toward the plate and he told me that it helped him "extend on the outside pitches." After watching some game film, it was clear that the pitchers were busting him inside and then going low and away, getting him out without ever throwing a strike! I put a two-by-four down the line that I wanted him to stride, setting it so he could only stride straight, instead of closed. With the board disabling his habit of striding toward the plate, he took twenty or so swings off of the tee.

After just a few minutes of practicing his new stride, he felt like he was able to get a lot more power from his body. The big difference came in games. He found that he had much better pitch selection because the outside pitches seemed farther away now that he wasn't diving toward them in his stride. Pitchers no longer saw a "chink in his armor" and were forced to throw good pitches. Plus he was able to turn his hips on the ball better, and drive the ball on the inside corner. The combination of stricter pitch selection and better hip rotation instantly gave him significantly more power and consistency. This is another example of how one change in positions can create a confluence of benefits.

60% RULE

The 60% Rule applies to two different aspects of how you allocate your weight in the Cushion. The first part applies to shifting your weight to your front side during your stride. As I mentioned before, to get the most power and consistency from your swing, you can't keep your weight on the back foot. You must shift at least 60% of your weight to your front foot in the stride.

The second part of the 60% Rule applies to how weight is distributed between your toes and your heels. It is best to keep 60% of your weight on your heels and 40% on your toes in the Cushion. Most players, however, put too much weight out on their toes. When they do this, they can't get the most from the spinning and straightening of the lower body in the forward swing because their center of gravity (around the waist) is not directly on top of their feet. Keeping 60% of your weight over your heels keeps your weight "stacked" so that when you spin and straighten to swing, you get the most force possible from your push against the ground.

Additionally, keeping 60% of your weight on your heels through the stride will give you better pitch selection. Players who fish for outside pitches often do so because they let their weight drift onto their toes as the pitch gets closer. If you train yourself to keep most of your weight on your heels, you simply can't reach the pitches that are too far outside. Eventually, you learn a tighter strike zone.

Albert Pujols is a great example of the second part of the 60% rule. He has great power and pitch selection because he keeps most of his weight on his heels in the stride. Next time you watch him bat, notice that when he takes the outside pitch, unlike most hitters, he doesn't lean towards the pitch. He has trained himself to keep most of his weight on his heels in the Cushion.

ENSURE A WHIPPING MOTION WITH THE BACK ARM

Ensure that there is space between the back elbow and your body in the Cushion. This will help you use the arms and bat in a whipping motion through the swing. Think of the way a sidearm pitcher first creates space between his back elbow and his body before tucking the elbow close to his side as he throws forward. Similarly, you should have adeqate space between your back elbow and body in the Cushion.

Similar to a throw motion, you should create space between your back elbow and body in the Cushion.

There should also be space between your hands and shoulder (your back elbow shouldn't be too bent). Again, think of a sidearm pitcher. If he loaded back with very little space between his hand and shoulder, he couldn't create leverage and get adequate whip from his arm.

There should also be space between your hands and back shoulder in the Cushion.

HEAD TURNED FULLY TOWARD PITCHER

In the Cushion, make your neck feel long and turn your head completely toward the pitcher. This will give you the feeling of being able to keep your head fairly still as you use hip and shoulder rotation to swing the bat. As neck flexibility increases, you will be able to increase the torque between your hips and shoulders without changing your head position.

CONQUER YOUR FEAR OF THE BASEBALL

A high school player, Michael, told me that he had always been afraid of the ball but didn't know why since he played football and didn't mind physical contact. When a curveball was headed towards him he would freeze. He came to me in hopes that I could help him conquer his fear of the curveball.

It was an important year for him. He was being recruited by colleges to play football and baseball, but wanted to pursue baseball. If he was going to earn a scholarship, this was the year. I explained to him that the problem was not in his head; it was not that he was afraid of the ball. The problem was in his positions.

You will often be surprised or fooled by a pitch as it leaves the pitcher's hand. It's just a natural reaction and there is no way to prevent it from happening. The key is to not let this reaction take you out of position. Even players who can hit the curveball well usually don't know when it's coming and are fooled when it's thrown. They can hit it despite being fooled because they've stayed in a good hitting position. Their mind flinches but their body stays ready to hit.

Therefore, the best way to conquer your "fear" of the baseball is to learn to stay in a good hitting position, even when you are surprised or fooled by the pitch. This is done by learning to achieve the Secondary Cushion. Remember, the pitcher's main objective is twofold: to throw strikes and to take you out of powerful and consistent positions. The curveball is usually the pitcher's best weapon because it makes the hitter physically flinch and get out of position. If you learn to achieve the Secondary Cushion, however, you will stay ready to hit should the ball curve back into the strike zone. If it doesn't curve, at least you are in the safest position from which to protect yourself. We'll talk about how to get hit by the pitch in the Guard section.

I worked with Michael to hone a good Cushion and Secondary Cushion by practicing them in front of a mirror. Then I had him practice his Cushion and Secondary Cushion off of a tee (Zero One Two Drill). His homework was to do this drill ten minutes a day.

It didn't take long for Michael to see the difference. He called a week later saying that he never felt so good at the plate. His pregame practice was just ten minutes of tee work, practicing his Cushion and Secondary Cushion positions. Michael would eventually move from the eighth spot to the fourth spot in the lineup just three weeks after our first meeting. He went on to lead the team in home runs and average, and earned a college scholarship.

Michael succeeded because he didn't try to fight his fear or change his attitude; he simply improved his positions and conditioned himself to flinch into a Secondary Cushion position. You are often going to flinch mentally, but it doesn't mean you have to be taken out of position.

IT'S CUSHION OR NOTHING

If you don't swing at a pitch, you should be paused in the Cushion. As you take batting practice, pitches at which you don't swing offer great opportunities to practice your Cushion. After the pitch passes, pause and wait one second, then look down and check your position (this is the one time it's ok to check your positioning during "moving ball" practice). You should be in a good Cushion or Secondary Cushion.

I often see players get impatient when the batting-practice pitcher can't find the strike zone. They get frustrated and start to drop their arms as the pitch is coming towards the plate. The player who does this is forming some very bad habits and missing a great opportunity to work on honing a solid Cushion position. Whether you are hitting soft-toss or batting practice, stay in your Cushion position until after the ball has passed you (or hit the ground in the case of soft toss).

THE TOE CUSHION VS. THE KNEE CUSHION

An increasing number of players are employing a Cushion position where their front heel remains off the ground as they wait on the pitch. This is not good. Since the Cushion position must get you to contact with the baseball as fast as possible, you should be fully grounded with your heel planted. If your front heel is off the ground, you aren't ready to swing because you must first land your heel. This means you will have to make your decision to swing much earlier. On fastballs you will often be late with a "heel up" Cushion and on breaking balls you will often swing at pitches out of the strike zone. Save yourself the trouble and be fully grounded in your Cushion by landing the front heel.

TIMING YOUR CUSHION IN THE ON-DECK CIRCLE

The Cushion and Secondary Cushion positions are your last line of defense against the pitcher changing speeds on you. The on-deck circle provides a great opportunity to begin to time them with the pitcher. Watch the pitcher's delivery and pitch, and then immediately close your eyes. Then physically time your stride as you visualize his delivery. Let three perfect (visualized) fastballs go by before taking swings. After the first three pitches, again, visualize three fastballs, but this time, add a swing.

After the first six pitches, start visualizing different pitches and locations– like curveballs and sliders, inside and outside, high and low. Achieve the Cushion or Secondary Cushion depending on the speed of the pitch. Hit outside pitches the opposite way, pull inside pitches, and hit pitches down the middle right back toward the pitcher. Visualize bad pitches in which you don't swing and hold a perfect Cushion or Secondary Cushion. Mix it up so that by the time you get to the plate, you have already seen it all and reacted properly. Visualizing in this way in the on-deck circle will greatly increase your odds of a successful at-bat.

SUMMARY – THE BENEFITS OF A GOOD CUSHION POSITION

With a good Cushion position, you will have more power because...

- ...the legs and back consist of very strong muscles that can whip the arms and bat with tremendous speed. The Cushion creates torque between your hips and shoulders and sets up your legs to provide the most possible bat speed.
- ...in order to get the most mass behind the bat as it travels through the hitting zone, you must use your bigger, stronger muscles to control the swing and let your arms and hands relax, connect to your body, and work like a whip. The Cushion sets you up to do so.

With a good Cushion position, you will have more consistency because...

- ...the bigger muscles in your legs and torso are easier to control than the smaller ones in your arms and hands. If your small muscles are in control, it's much more difficult to hold a checked swing. The Cushion sets up your bigger muscles to be in control, which allows you to time your swing more accurately with the pitch.
- ...by fully coiling your bigger muscles, you are creating the shortest amount of time between your decision to swing and contact with the baseball.
- ...letting the big muscles control the swing naturally increases your Area of Impact. The opposite of using your bigger muscles to control the swing would be firing your hands out in a punching motion toward the ball. Many coaches advocate this "extension" or "stay inside the ball" approach, but it creates a very small AOI.
- ...setting the bigger muscles up to control the swing will enable your arms to drop close to your side and stay connected to your body through the swing. This naturally restricts your bat reach, which improves your pitch selection.

THE SLOT POSITION

In the Slot position, you have just decided to swing at the pitch: your front knee begins to straighten, your hips start to rotate, and your arms are loose - going along for the ride. The straightening of your front knee and the rotating of your hips controls the entire move, as your back elbow falls close to your side, and the bat momentarily fires toward the pitcher from behind you, creating "bat lag." *The Slot position occurs on video when the bat flattens out prior to its forward rotation into the hitting zone.*

The Slot position is a personal favorite for me. A good Slot position is great to see on video because it is an incredibly dynamic position. It is also a position that plainly shows how well the player uses the bigger muscles in his legs and hips to control the swing. If he incorrectly uses just his upper body and arms to swing, the hands fire outward prematurely and become disconnected from the body. However, if he uses his bigger muscles properly to control the swing, the back elbow "slots" nicely to his side, "catching a ride" on his hip rotation.

BAT LAG AND ANGLE L

Maximizing bat lag in the Slot position, before the bat travels through the hitting zone, is a change in the swing that will differentiate hitters in the future from today's hitters. Far too many players at high levels of baseball do not take advantage of this.

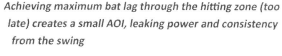

More bat lag translates into more bat speed. It's important, however, to achieve your maximum bat lag early, in the Slot position, *before* the bat enters the hitting zone, so it doesn't affect your AOI. Players who prematurely extend their hands out toward the ball (stay-inside-the-ball-approach) achieve maximum bat lag too late.

Achieving maximum bat lag through the hitting zone (too late) creates a small AOI, leaking power and consistency from the swing

If you tend to "roll over" on pitches and pull weak ground balls or push weak fly balls to the opposite field, you are achieving maximum bat lag too late into the forward swing. While many hitters have performed well achieving a late bat lag, they did so in spite of it. They could have had much more power and consistency by achieving maximum bat lag earlier, in the Slot position. **Measure your bat lag in the Slot position by connecting the dots from your front elbow, to the knob of the bat, to the barrel. This is Angle L.**

See how low you can get Angle L in the Slot position without compromising grip consistency. Somewhere between 60 and 90 degrees is good.

When achieving bat lag in the Slot position, there will be a slight pull of the barrel toward the pitcher (from behind you). From here, the barrel of the bat will fire outward into the hitting zone, creating a long AOI.

Maximum bat lag should occur in the Slot position, measured by Angle L.

SLOTTING THE BACK ELBOW

When the back elbow drops close to the player's side in the Slot position, the hitter accomplishes three things. First, the bat is dropped on a single, flat plane that is close to matching, if not exactly intersecting, the path of the pitch. This increases the hitter's odds of making contact, as opposed to a swing that starts in a downward motion and only flattens out (if at all) in the latter portion of the hitting zone.

Second, by dropping the elbow close to the player's side, the bat gets "on-plane" early, creating more speed through the hitting zone. Think of a racecar: the longer the racecar stays on a straightaway, the more speed it can generate. Similarly, the faster you get the bat on the same plane as your rotating body, the more speed it can generate through the zone.

Some hitting coaches advocate a swing where the bat changes planes as it travels through the zone. Mike Epstein advocates a swing that goes "down-level-up." However, a swing that changes planes can never pick up as much speed as a swing that stays on the same plane from beginning to end.

And third, slotting the back elbow sets up the hitter to be more connected at Impact, transferring more mass into the ball. The combination of bat mass and bat speed adds significantly to the overall bat force at Impact.

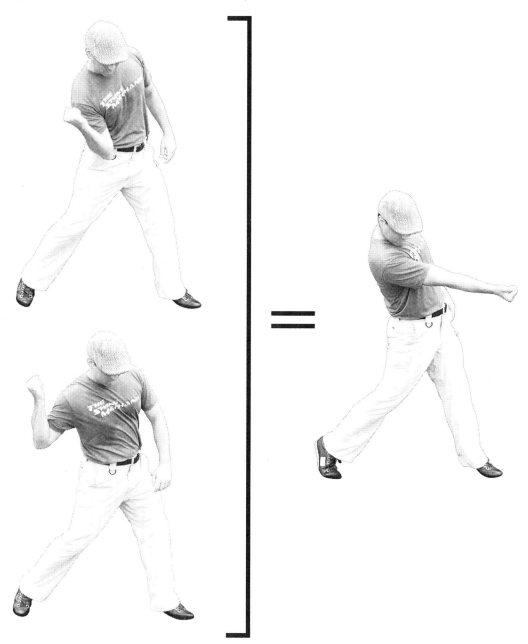

Letting the back elbow get in front of the hip or too high when starting the forward swing will give you a poor Impact position whereby the back arm is too extended.

It is important that the back elbow be at the player's side and not in front of his hip. If the back elbow is in front of the hip in the Slot, the hitter will get "stuck" and will have to slow his body rotation and extend his back arm prematurely in order to square the bat to the ball. This leaks power and consistency from his swing. The same is true if the elbow is too far away from the body in the Slot position.

A Major League player who "slots" his back elbow nicely to begin the forward swing is Lance Berkman.

A SHORT BAT MEANS A FLATTER PLANE

Earlier I mentioned that letting your elbow drop to your side drops the bat on a flatter, more level plane, improving your power and consistency. You can drop the bat on an even flatter plane by rotating your back forearm skyward in the Slot position. This will appear on video as a "short bat."   Again, the earlier the plane of your bat matches the plane of your body rotation, the more bat speed you can generate through the hitting zone and the better odds you have of making contact with the baseball. Therefore, a "short bat" further improves your power and consistency.

A long bat means that the bat has not dropped on plane.

A short bat indicates that the bat has dropped on plane.

While the arms and hands can guide the bat into this flatter position, it results primarily from using your legs and hips to control the swing. A good way to ensure that you do this is by having a majority of your center of gravity directly stacked on top of your heels (second part of the 60% Rule).

HANDS OUTSIDE OF BODY

When the hands appear inside of the body in the Slot position, the hitter is employing a punch motion with his back arm. When the hands appear outside of the body in the Slot position, the hitter is using the much more effective throw, or whipping, motion.

The hands inside the body in the Slot position is not good because it indicates that the hitter is employing a punch motion with his back arm.

Think of throwing a baseball. You can throw the ball much faster using your back rotator cuff as opposed to using your triceps in a shot-put motion. The same principle applies to the swing: you will have much more power and consistency using the throw motion.

To recap, immediately after you begin your forward swing, you should feel your arms drop to your side. As they drop, your elbow should tuck to your side and your back forearm turns to face skyward. This move drops the bat on a flatter plane and places your hands outside of your body in the Slot position.

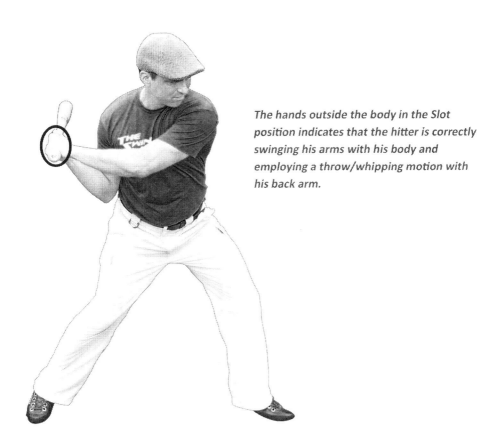

The hands outside the body in the Slot position indicates that the hitter is correctly swinging his arms with his body and employing a throw/whipping motion with his back arm.

PSA ESTABLISHED AND REMAINS CONSISTENT TO FINISH

Your Pitcher's Perspective Spine Angle (PSA) is your spine tilt as seen from the pitcher's perspective. Starting in the Slot, you will tilt, straighten, or maintain your PSA depending on the height of the pitch. On low pitches, your spine will tilt downward. On high pitches, your spine becomes more vertical.

In your Cushion, you should achieve a "middle of the road" PSA, one that enables you to quickly adjust to high and low strikes. Once you begin your forward swing, you should maintain or change your PSA to hit the pitch. When tilting your PSA to hit a low pitch, especially low and outside, make sure that you don't get too much weight onto your toes. The second part of the 60% Rule still applies into the Slot position and on low pitches when your PSA tilts downward. With practice, you will eventually know your PSA range, and knowing your PSA range will naturally improve your pitch selection.

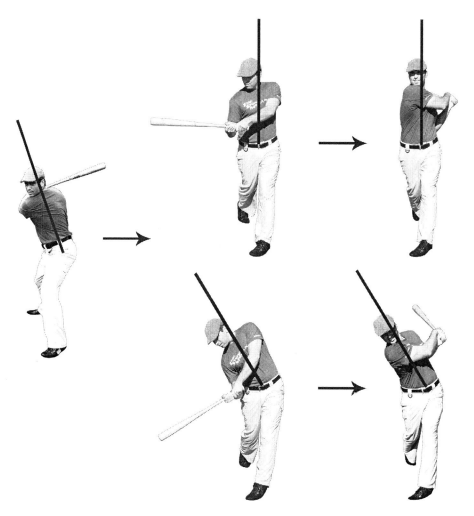

Your PSA should change in the Slot according to the height of the pitch and stay consistent to the end of the swing.

SPINE ANGLE STRAIGHT UP AND DOWN

Those who advocate the rotational hitting method believe that the player should lean back through the swing. Mike Epstein writes, "When the player's front heel drops, his rear shoulder must begin to dip at nearly the same instant." However, exactly *none* of the greatest hitters in the history of baseball leaned back through the forward swing. If the hitter's front shoulder appears lower from the front angle, it's probably because he is rotating around a tilted PSA, not because he is dipping his back shoulder.

When the spine tilts back through the swing, the hitter loses power and consistency.

It just doesn't make sense to lean back through the swing. Have you ever seen a boxer throw a punch and lean backwards, away from his target? Of course not. Other than having had improper instruction, there are two more reasons why hitters may lean back at the start the forward swing.

The first possibility is that their back arm prematurely extended the knob of the bat outward toward the ball (stay-inside-the-ball approach), keeping the barrel from entering the hitting zone. Since the barrel travels through most of the hitting zone without squaring to the baseball, leaning back is a way for the hitter to create more room to square the barrel.

The second possibility is that they didn't shift their weight in the stride, creating a swing with only the upper body. When this happens, the force of their arms pushing toward the ball pushes back on their upper body, causing them to get "pushed" backwards through the swing.

STRAIGHTENING THE FRONT LEG

In the Slot, the front leg has started to straighten, snapping the hips open. The hips begin to rotate just a fraction of a second before the shoulders. The shoulders will catch up to the hips in the next position, Impact.

THE IMPACT POSITION

Positional Hitting is about changing the physics of your swing to increase both power and consistency. It is possible however, to hit well and not achieve certain key positions of the swing, except when it comes to Impact. Impact is, by far, the most important position. To hit with both power and consistency, you must have a good Impact position. *Impact is measured when you make contact (or would have made contact) with the baseball.*

Former Major Leaguer Albert Belle, who hit 50 home runs for the Cleveland Indians in 1995, had a below average Slot position but made up for it with great angles at Impact. The best hitter ever, Babe Ruth, had an average Cushion position but the best Impact position I've ever measured. He also still holds most of the offensive records.

The angles at Impact are most directly correlated to power and consistency. Without making a change to your Impact position, you are the same hitter no matter how hard you work. I often refer to the Impact position as the "thumbprint of your swing." Just as a thumbprint can determine the identification of a criminal, the Impact position can determine the ultimate potential of a hitter.

THE CSR FORMULA FOR MEASURING YOUR SWING MECHANICS

There are two key angles that are measured in the Impact position, Angle E and Angle W. **Angle E is measured by connecting the dots from the middle of your back shoulder, to the tip of your back elbow, to the middle of your top hand on the bat. Angle W is measured by connecting the dots from the tip of your back elbow, to the middle of your top hand, to the center of the bat barrel.** The two angles share a common line: from the tip of the elbow to the hand.

The two key angles at Impact, Angle E and Angle W

Angle E indicates the amount of mass behind the hit. The more bent your back elbow, the more body mass transferred to the ball. A smaller Angle E means more mass and a larger Angle E means less mass. Because you want to have the most possible mass transferred to the ball at Impact, you want Angle E to be small. Note that the back elbow should be by your side, not in *front* of your side, at Impact.

Angle W measures how released the bat is at Impact. If the bat is more released, then it has had more distance to increase its acceleration. Therefore, a large Angle W means more speed and a small Angle W means less speed. Since force = mass x acceleration, the combination of a small Angle E and a large Angle W increases the overall force transferred to the ball, the key to a good Impact position, and also the key to a great swing.

On outside pitches, which are hit deeper in the zone (closer to the catcher), you will not be able to get your Angle W as high as on inside pitches. Inside pitches are hit farther out in front of the plate (closer to the pitcher) and therefore Angle W can be larger. This is the reason that players are able to hit inside pitches harder. Your goal remains, however, to get your Angle W as high as possible and Angle E as small as possible, regardless of the pitch location.

Since the Impact position is the most important of all, the Cevallos Swing Rating equation (CSR), measured at Impact, yields an overall rating of your swing mechanics. Obtain your CSR score by plugging your Angle E and Angle W into the following CSR equation:

$$CSR = 3(180 - E) + W$$

The best Impact position in the game today belongs to Albert Pujols. The best Angle E and W combination ever was achieved by Babe Ruth.

Your CSR on tee swings, without consciously making changes, will typically only vary by single digits, if at all. It will vary more in your game swings. If you want to measure your mechanics for a particular game, get the average score for all of your swings to calculate your score for the day. Here are CSR scores that I've obtained of former Major League players during games, along with their lifetime SLG and OPS.

	CSR	SLG	OPS
Babe Ruth	463	.690	1.1638
Ted Williams	429	.634	1.1155
Hank Aaron	422	.555	.928
Albert Belle	393	.564	.933
Harmon Killebrew	386	.509	.884
Bernie Williams	381	.477	.858
Wade Boggs	354	.443	.858
Tony Gwynn	321	.459	.847
Pete Rose	318	.409	.784
Don Mattingly	313	.471	.830
Rickey Henderson	296	.419	.820

List of Major League Players and their CSR scores, SLG and OPS

Your CSR score is not only indicative of your power. A high CSR score also says that your barrel entered the hitting zone early and stayed there for a long time, creating a long AOI and increasing your consistency. This is how the greatest hitters maintained high levels of both power and consistency. They had the sweetest and most effortless swings and made it look so easy because they had a high CSR and the rest took care of itself.

In a low CSR swing, the player pushes the bat knob into the hitting zone, creating a small AOI and very little power.

In a high CSR swing, the body rotation swings the bat, letting the barrel whip into the hitting zone early, creating more force behind the bat and a long AOI.

Obtaining Angle W on outside pitches will be difficult because of the camera angle. For this reason, it is best to obtain your CSR scores off of a tee when hitting down-the-middle or inside pitches because you can get a good read on your Angle W.

One of my goals when writing this book was to finally provide players a way to accurately assess their own swing mechanics. So many books on hitting leave players more confused than anything. Mike Epstein writes in his book, "The natural swing starts in the vicinity of the rear shoulder, initially follows a downward path, levels off approximately four inches in front of the lead knee, and then begins its upslope to finish in the vicinity of the front shoulder." Aside from the fact that he is advocating a swing that changes planes through the hitting zone, I disagree with using words like "approximately" and "vicinity" because indefinite terms don't allow the player to adequately assess his own mechanics.

With the CSR equation, players can measure the effectiveness of their swing mechanics with precision. For many of my students, it becomes a game within the game to get their CSR as high as possible when hitting off of a tee.

THE FRONT ARM CLOSE TO CHEST

Your front arm should stay tight to your chest at Impact. Why? Think back to the equation of Force: Force = mass x acceleration. With the front arm tight to the chest, more mass will be transferred from your body through the bat and ultimately will deliver more force to the ball at Impact.

Less mass, and therefore less force, is delivered to the ball with the front arm away from the chest at Impact.

More mass, and therefore more force, is delivered to the ball with the front arm tight to the chest at Impact.

VERTICAL SPINE ANGLE

As I stated in the Slot section, your spine angle must remain vertical through your swing. Again, imagine if a boxer was leaning back when punching his opponent; he wouldn't be very effective. The same is true in hitting. Ensure that you are transferring the most force possible to the ball by making sure that your spine angle is straight-up-and-down at Impact.

THE HIPS, SHOULDERS AND FRONT KNEE

It is the snapping straight of the front knee that helps to fire the hips open with great speed. The front knee, at Impact, should be straight, or snapping straight. The shoulders have just caught up with the hips and the two are aligned.

A LOW CSR, BAD IMPACT POSITION

A bad Impact position (low CSR) occurs when the player's back arm is extended and his bat is unreleased. Coaches who advocate "extending the arms at contact" or "staying inside the ball," are teaching players to hone a bad Impact position.

A low CSR, bad Impact position

There is also a lack of body turn in a low CSR Impact position. This happens when the back arm prematurely fires outward toward the ball, slowing body rotation. As long as the back arm remains well bent and relaxed as the body rotates, the body can continue to turn, hitting through the ball - not at it.

THE DELIVERY POSITION

In the Delivery position, your hips should be in the same position as they are at Impact, facing the pitcher. The shoulders, however, have now passed the hips. The spine angle stays vertical and the PSA that you established in the Slot should be the same.

The Delivery position will give you a good indication of...

- ...the amount that your big muscles controlled the swing.
- ...the length of your AOI.

The Delivery position is measured when the top-hand arm is facing 2 o'clock for righties and 10 o'clock for lefties. The key angle that you will measure in the Delivery is Angle D, and it is a good indication of how well you used your big muscles as the "engine" for your swing. **Angle D is obtained by connecting the dots from your top hand shoulder, to the middle of your top hand where it meets the bat, to the center of the barrel.** Ideally Angle D is close to or at 180 degrees, meaning these three points will connect in virtually a straight line. The smaller Angle D is, the more you flipped the bat through the zone rather than using the big muscles in your legs and torso to control the swing.

In a bad Delivery position, the shoulders stop rotating, the back arm fires outward and the bat flips through the zone, producing a small Angle D.

BACK SHOULDER DRIVES FORWARD AND AROUND

From the Slot position, let the hands whip the barrel of the bat into the hitting zone quickly with your body rotation, without extending your top-hand arm. Once you do that, just let your hips and shoulders continue their rotation. By the time you get to the Delivery position, your top-hand arm will have just extended straight, and will be in line with the bat. From the Delivery position, the bat will pull your top-hand shoulder around to Finish. If you are not used to this movement, the feeling will be that your top-hand shoulder fires forward and around from Slot to Finish.

Players with a low Angle D, perhaps below 100 degrees, have prematurely extended their back arm out toward the ball to begin the swing. This keeps the barrel away from the zone for too long, creating a short AOI. In an attempt to correct this problem, the hitter will slow his shoulder rotation, tilt his spine angle back, and force the barrel into the zone with the muscles in the forearms and hands.

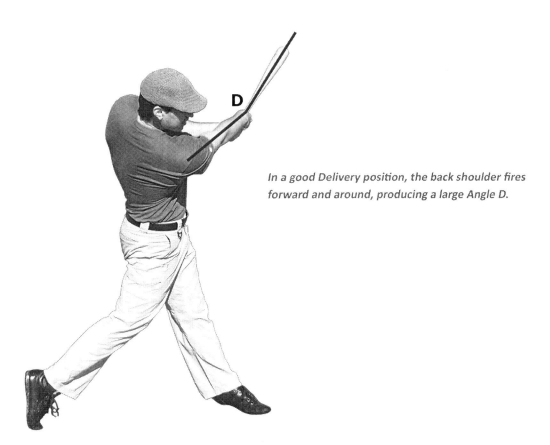

In a good Delivery position, the back shoulder fires forward and around, producing a large Angle D.

TOP HAND WORKS UNDER BOTTOM HAND

Many people have commented about how Chase Utley cuts his swing off so short and is still able to hit so well. Utley has a swing where he practically stops in the Delivery position. However, rather than hitting well in spite of his short swing, in a way, he hits well *because* of it. Utley's swing, like the swing of all great hitters, is one in which his top hand slowly rotates over his bottom hand after Impact. This action ensures a long AOI and more bat force. The opposite of this would be to flip your top hand over your bottom hand through the zone and achieve a small Angle D.

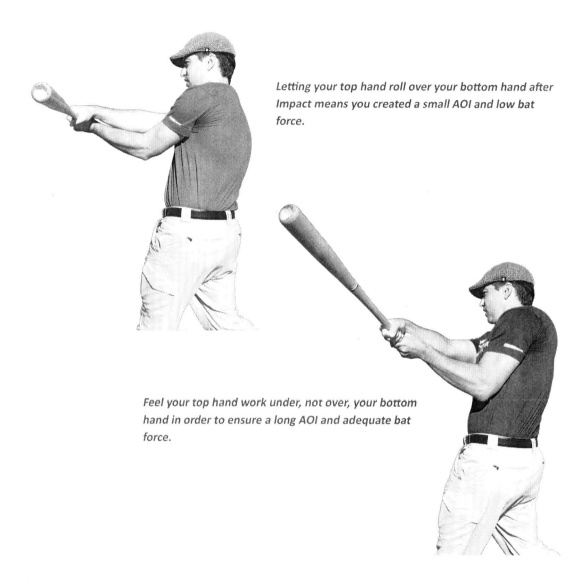

Letting your top hand roll over your bottom hand after Impact means you created a small AOI and low bat force.

Feel your top hand work under, not over, your bottom hand in order to ensure a long AOI and adequate bat force.

To prevent your top hand from quickly flipping over your bottom hand through the swing, let your top hand work under, not over, your bottom hand in the Delivery position. When you do this, your bottom-hand elbow will fold in order to allow the bat to continue to Finish. This will ensure that you hit the ball with the big muscles and not the flip of the wrists.

THE FINISH POSITION

The Finish position is measured when the momentum of the forward swing has stopped. From Delivery to Finish, your bat should take a wide arc. The wide arc shows that you used your big muscles to swing the bat, producing a long AOI and adequate bat force through the hitting zone.

In a good swing, a wide arc is created by the bat from Delivery to Finish

BALANCED FINISH ENSURES EFFICIENCY

A balanced Finish provides a good indication of the efficiency with which a player swings. The player who throws his hands toward the ball instead of using his body to whip the bat will often finish off-balanced. Therefore, I tell my students to hold a balanced Finish position for three seconds when practicing. If they can do this, chances are that the force of the swing was generated by the legs and torso, rather than from the arms.

BALANCED FINISH IMPROVES PITCH SELECTION

A balanced Finish position will improve your pitch selection. Rogers Hornsby, arguably the best right handed hitter of all time, said that the most important thing for a hitter to do was to get a good pitch to hit. Coaches routinely remind players of this prior to an at-bat, but just *telling* a hitter to get a good pitch to hit is worthless. The best way to improve your pitch selection is to hone swing positions that restrict your bat-reach.

If you get too much weight out on your toes through the swing, you will chase pitches that are too far outside and you will finish off-balanced. Ensuring that you finish balanced improves your pitch selection because the less you lean toward the plate through the swing, the less you can reach pitches outside of the strike zone. Therefore, a balanced Finish improves pitch selection through swing restriction.

VERTICAL SPINE ANGLE

I often see players finish with their back tilting backward toward the catcher. This is an indication that the arms and hands overworked through the swing, not allowing the bigger muscles to supply the power. From Slot to Finish, ensure that your spine angle is straight up and down.

As for your PSA, it should be at the same angle that you established in the Slot. When practicing off of a tee, make sure you finish with a PSA that is right for the height of the pitch that you are working on.

Check to ensure that your spine angle is straight up and down at Finish

THE HIPS, SHOULDERS, AND KNEE

Without even noticing, many hitters get in the habit of not completely finishing the rotation of their swing. Right handed hitters especially, because they are headed to first base, are prone to this. Over time, a hitter who goes down this path will use less and less of the big and strong muscles in the legs and torso and wind up waving weakly at the pitches with just his arms. This hitter, without even noticing, has neglected his Finish position and he will pay dearly for it.

It's important to hold your Finish position when practicing off of a tee. To ensure that you've used your big muscles to control the swing, check that your belt buckle and back shoulder are facing the pitcher and your front knee is snapped straight. It is difficult to finish in this position and *not* have produced a very powerful and consistent swing.

THE GUARD POSITION

The Guard position is the best position in which to get hit by a pitch. Instead of jumping out of the way of pitches, in the future, players will simply wear more padding in the right places and use the much more effective Guard position. The Guard position not only protects you from errant pitches, it allows you to get the most out of the good ones as well.

Traditionally, when a player prepares to get hit by the baseball, he does one of two things that simultaneously get him out of position, make him more vulnerable to injury, and hurt his hitting performance. They are:

1. *Keep the majority of weight on the back foot, making it impossible to swing with the bigger, stronger muscles in the legs and torso.*
2. *Align the hips with his shoulders, losing the source of torque and power in the swing.*

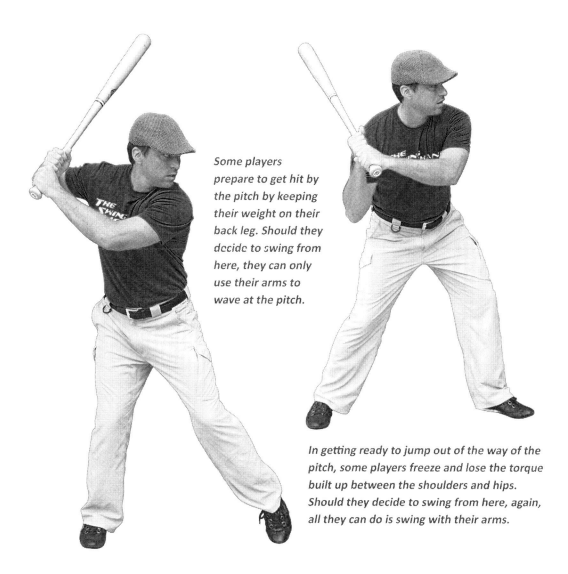

Some players prepare to get hit by the pitch by keeping their weight on their back leg. Should they decide to swing from here, they can only use their arms to wave at the pitch.

In getting ready to jump out of the way of the pitch, some players freeze and lose the torque built up between the shoulders and hips. Should they decide to swing from here, again, all they can do is swing with their arms.

These two actions are typically called "buckling the knees." If you buckle your knees and the pitch is a ball, then you are ok. If you buckle your knees and the pitch is a strike, you will want to find the nearest rock to crawl under. Buckling the knees can be quite embarrassing.

The key to never buckling your knees is honing your Cushion and Guard positions. As we discussed in the section on the Cushion, flinching properly is a learned skill. For balls that appear to be out of the strike zone early in the flight of the pitch, stay in your Cushion and wait to see what happens. If you are certain that the ball is going to hit you, assume the Guard position. The Guard position will provide you with the quickest and safest refuge.

Even the best players in baseball don't seem to have a set position for when the ball is coming towards them. This is something that will be a big difference between the hitters of today and hitters in the future. In time, as OPS becomes more important than batting average, players will have more incentive to get hit by the pitch. After all, getting a HBP is often just as good for the team as a base hit.

In more physical sports, the need to practice protective positions is obvious. Mixed Martial Arts (MMA) fighters learn early on that if they are going to succeed, they have to protect themselves by practicing effective guard positions. Can you imagine an MMA fighter not having a method for blocking punches and kicks? He would get hit far too often to make it very far in the sport. Therefore, a good amount of their practice time is spent honing these guard positions because they know that improving their defense allows them to get the most out of their offense. The same is true in hitting.

The Guard position is just as important for when you don't get hit by the pitch as it is for when you do. Although getting hit by a pitch is pretty rare, it is always in the back of the hitter's mind. Therefore, it becomes a factor on every single pitch. If you hone your Guard position, you will be able to completely block that concern out of your mind and focus 100% on hitting the baseball.

PICK UP OFF-SPEED PITCHES BETTER

The Guard position will enable you to see the ball longer than the player who needs the time to jump out of the way. When players say they didn't "see the ball well," I translate that as: "they didn't stay in a good hitting position long enough." Seeing the ball and staying in a good hitting position go hand in hand. Often what feels like "not seeing the ball well" is really "not being in position to hit."

The Guard position, because you can achieve it quickly, lets you stay in a good hitting position longer before protecting yourself. It can be achieved quickly because it is the Cushion (or Secondary Cushion) with just two quick modifications: your head is turned away from the pitcher and your front shoulder is lifted.

PROTECTS YOU BETTER THAN JUMPING OUT OF THE WAY

For all the work players do to get out of the way of a pitch, I find it ironic that they are actually making themselves more, not less, vulnerable. You must assume that you don't have enough time to get out of the way of the pitch because...well...you don't. This applies even more to players at the higher levels where pitchers are throwing 80, 90, and even 100 mph. Most of the moving players do, moves more delicate parts of their body right into the path of the ball. If they hone the Guard position, they may still get hit, but not in areas that cause the most pain and injury.

Once you hone a good Guard position, you can even put padding on areas that are exposed in the Guard, further protecting yourself.

OFFENSIVE MIND

It's a funny thing about baseball that the team on offense often has a more defensive attitude than the team on the field. It's probably because the defense starts off with the ball. I believe that honing the Guard position will shift the offensive mentality more towards the hitters, where it belongs.

If you know in the back of your mind that you not only have to hit the baseball but also maneuver your body out of the way if it comes toward you, you will not be fully at ease in the box. You will be amazed at how much harder you can swing by honing a good Guard position. It allows you to be more offensive.

EVERYTHING ELSE IS CUSHION

There are two reasons why everything but the head and front shoulder in the Guard is exactly like the Cushion. The first is for quickness. The Guard only requires that you simultaneously turn your head and lift your shoulder, a move that can be performed in an instant. Like in any sport, a good guard must be quick.

The second is more luck than anything – it just so happens that the Cushion, the best position from which to swing, is very close to the best position in which to get hit. While the Guard does expose the meaty part of your back and shoulder, it covers the delicate parts of your body. Sure it may sting if you get hit in the Guard, but it is highly unlikely that you won't be able to make the jog down to first base and stay in the game.

CHAPTER CHALLENGE

Focus, Thank, Analyze and Train. It is unfortunate that many athletes don't understand the real purpose of competition. They see the opponent as the enemy and that competition is just an opportunity to show how good they are. Viewing competition like this will blind you to opportunities for progress. The less concerned you are about what others think, the more attention you can put into improving.

For the next month, when competing against someone in anything, see it as an opportunity to improve. During the competition, focus 100% on the task at hand. Afterwards, thank your opponent for the challenge. Then analyze where you could have done better and what you could do to improve. Lastly, spend time practicing, even if just a few moments, the very thing that you could improve upon. This is a good series of events to follow in order to improve quickly and see competition from the right perspective: focus, thank your opponent, analyze and train.

Viewing competition as an opportunity to grow takes practice. In time, viewing competition in this way will accelerate your hitting improvement. I've seen players from other cultures bow prior to stepping into the batter's box. This seems like a much better view of the challenge of hitting and of competition as a whole. The purpose of competition is to learn and grow. If you see it as such, success will take care of itself.

CHAPTER THREE

POSITIONAL TRAINING
CHANGING POSITIONS BY
CHANGING MOVEMENTS

*"What's the difference between a hero and a coward? There ain't no difference.
Inside they're both exactly alike. They're both scared of dying or getting hurt.
It's what the hero does that makes him a hero,
what the other guy doesn't do makes him a coward."*

—Cus D'Amato

It's one thing to understand the key positions and a completely different matter to achieve them in your own swing. I'll tell you up front, you can't force the key positions. The key positions are achieved through the right *movements*. It just takes one look at the swing of Ken Griffey, Ted Williams or Babe Ruth to see that the greatest swings are not "forced." They are effortless.

The most effective movements are comfortable and natural. It's ok to move in an uncoordinated fashion at first, but in time your swing should look and feel natural and fluid. The most effective baseball swings are also the prettiest.

I have designed the drills in this chapter to let the player "discover" the right movements on his own. They have led to the most immediate and drastic improvement in my students and they can do the same for you.

I once heard it said that good players practice until they get it right and great players practice until they can't get it wrong. This same concept should apply to training your swing. Even after you feel the proper swing movement, you will still need to repeat it enough in practice so that in the heat of the game your body resorts to the movement that is most familiar. Remember that the pitcher's goal is to pull you out of good hitting positions. The more you practice the proper movements, the harder it becomes for him to do that.

Do the drills for as long or short as you want. There is no program that you have to stick by. Set up stations and rotate through the drills or focus on one drill for thirty minutes. Work by yourself or in groups. Do them when you can, for as long as you can; just do them. And it's ok to get creative and modify the drills in ways that you think might help you.

The more that you feel the movements that produce the key positions, the sooner you will achieve them in games and begin hitting with more power and consistency. Put to rest the notion that you aren't practicing unless you see live pitching. Remember that the main challenge in hitting lies in your positions. Just ten minutes of positional training is better than two hours of batting practice.

IMPACT BAG DRILL

PART 1

The IB Drill, part 1

Assume your stance and set up to a heavy punching bag like you would a batting tee. Let your legs and torso have complete control of the swing. Shift your weight back and wind up your hips, then step forward and unwind your hips, letting the arms and bat whip into the bag, stopping you at Impact. Pause and check your Impact position.

The main objective in the IB Drill is to achieve a good Impact position using your legs and torso to whip the arms and bat. Forget the notion that this is a baseball swing for now. Your only three objectives are to...

1. ...control the swing with your legs and hips.
2. ...let the barrel of the bat rotate into the hitting zone quickly from the Slot position.
3. ...end in a good Impact position with the bag.

Once you can achieve a good Impact position, repeat the motion paying particular attention to the movement of the "engine" of your swing (legs and hips). Notice how your legs and hips must move in order to finish in a good Impact position. Doing the IB Drill in front of a mirror can help you see this. Notice the exact timing and sequence of your legs and hips, how your weight shifts and your body rotates, and how your arms drop loosely to your side to begin the swing. This is the magic move. Pay attention to it.

Tips for The Impact Bag Drill, Part 1

- With your legs and hips in control of your swing, your back elbow will naturally fall to your side as you start your forward swing.
- At first, players often overwork their back arm, prematurely extending it toward the bag as they have always done in their swing. If you are having this problem, focus on keeping the same bend in your back elbow from your stance all the way to Impact. This takes away the ability of your back arm to supply any power and forces your legs and torso to rotate your body, and the wrists to remain loose and whip the bat into the bag.
- When checking your Impact position, also check that you maintained a CLS grip.

PART 2

The IB Drill, part 2

Use the same motion that produced a good Impact position in the first part, but instead of hitting a heavy bag, hit a baseball off of a tee and continue to Finish. Pause in the Finish for three seconds.

Tips for The Impact Bag Drill, Part 2

- Visualize the ball on the tee as being the bag. Again, erase the notion that this is a baseball swing. Your only three goals are to give control of the swing to your legs and hips, get the barrel rotating quickly into the hitting zone from the Slot position, and achieve a good Impact position.
- It may feel like your top hand is being pulled around to Finish. This is because you are using your entire body to swing. Allow this feeling to happen.

THE SLOT DRILL

PART 1

Slot Drill, part 1

If you are having trouble achieving the Slot position in your swing, the Slot Drill will help. Hit balls off of a tee starting in the Slot. The inability to achieve the Slot position happens for two reasons: your arms are overworking and your body is under-working. By presetting your arms in the Slot, you are forcing your legs and hips to control the forward swing, as they should.

Tips For The Slot Drill, Part 1

- Focus on hitting the ball with your body rotation.
- Feel your back elbow stay at your side until after Impact.
- Let the barrel of the bat whip outward, into the hitting zone, at the start of the movement.

PART 2

Slot Drill, part 2

In the second part of the Slot drill, take regular swings off of a tee, letting your arms *drop* into the Slot position. The second part is designed to achieve the Slot position within the entire swing.

Tips for The Slot Drill, Part 2

- The slotting of the back elbow occurs because a majority of your center of gravity, located around your waist, is directly above your heels, giving your legs and hips control of the swing. Feeling a majority of your weight on your heels through the stride will enable you to slot your back elbow to begin the forward swing.
- Feel bat lag by letting the bat whip towards the pitcher from behind you, before firing outward into the hitting zone.

CUSHION DRILL

PART 1

Cushion Drill, part 1

The Cushion drill will help you "tighten up" the big muscle movement that you achieved in the Impact Bag and Slot drills. In your batting stance, hold the bat behind your shoulders so the knob of the bat points in the direction of the pitcher.

Go from your stance, into your stride, and stop in the Cushion. The knob of the bat should face down the first base line for righties and third base line for lefties; the front knee and foot should face the second baseman for righties and the shortstop for lefties. Once you've achieved a good Cushion, finish the swing, using your hips to "throw" your shoulders. At Finish, the knob of the bat should be facing in the direction of the catcher. Hold your Finish for three seconds.

Tips for The Cushion Drill, Part 1

- Keep in mind the TF Triple S sequence (see The Fall Position). The point of this drill is to work on your lower body movement, the "engine" of the swing.
- Use a similar motion with your legs and hips that you achieved during the Impact Bag Drill. In the Cushion Drill, you are just tightening it up.
- To keep you tall in the Fall portion of your stride, keep your back leg rigid (don't increase the bend in your back knee) when shifting your weight back. As you fall forward, be patient and let gravity drop you onto your front leg.
- Don't move too quickly from the Cushion to Finish. Speed is not as important as power with this move. Build this move from the ground up.

PART 2

The second part of the Cushion drill is just like the first, except that you will not pause in your Cushion to check your position. You will practice achieving both your Cushion and

Secondary Cushion in the context of a fluid swing movement. Hold your finish for three seconds.

Tips for the Cushion Drill, Part 2

- Again, don't rush through the forward swing. Feel like you are moving at 70% speed. Players tend to move too fast from the Cushion or Secondary Cushion to Finish when doing this drill. Form is more important than speed here. The big muscles build energy from the ground up by moving rhythmically.
- Feel your center of gravity stacked over your legs by keeping 60% of your weight on your heels and 40% on your toes through your stride. As you spin and straighten to finish the swing, you will feel the power that this gives you.

ZERO ONE TWOS

In a "zero," you will stride and swing in one fluid motion, simulating a well timed stride, most likely a fastball.

In a "one" or "two," you will achieve the Secondary Cushion position (for either one or two seconds) before finishing the swing.

- Place a ball on a tee and get into your stance
- Make swings, pausing for one or two seconds (a "one" or a "two") in your Secondary Cushion or passing through your Cushion with no pause at all ("zero").
- Hold your finish for three seconds.

The Zero One Two Drill makes your swing "game ready." The "zero," the "one," and the "two," indicate the seconds you will spend in your Cushion or Secondary Cushion position before starting the forward swing. The "one" and "two" simulate a slightly mistimed stride, likely an off-speed pitch, where you wait momentarily in your Secondary Cushion before swinging. A "zero" simulates a well timed stride, in which you smoothly pass through the Cushion (no Secondary Cushion) and into the forward swing.

For the "ones" and "twos," you are purposefully "fooling yourself" by practicing your Secondary Cushion. Your goal is to make game swings fluid even when fooled on the pitch.

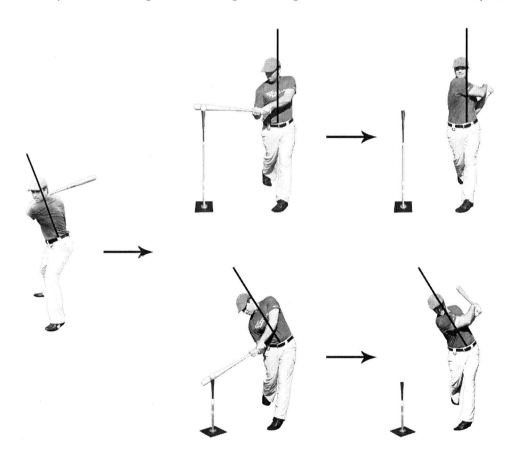

Zero One Twos are a good opportunity to practice adjusting your PSA by working on different height pitches.

Tips for the Zero One Two Drill

- Try not to be completely still at any point in your "ones" or "twos." Do this by gradually increasing the amount of weight on your front leg and the bend in your front knee, but maintaining the torque in your hips and shoulders.

The strike zone exists on a diagonal line

- Use this drill for your Perfection Filming.
- Zero One Twos are a great opportunity to work on your Guard. At random times, get into your Guard position instead of continuing into the forward swing.
- Work on all types of locations: down-the-middle; inside and outside; and high, low and medium height. Practice all of the above in all the various combinations. When working on high and low pitches, change your PSA in the Slot and maintain that PSA until Finish.
- To determine where to place the tee for different pitch locations (outside, inside, and down the middle), assume your stance and stride into your Cushion. From there, go slowly to Impact and simulate a good Impact position. Position yourself relative to the ball so that when you achieve a perfect Impact position, the ball is exactly on the bat's sweet spot. As you work on inside and outside locations, you will find that the strike zone is a diagonal line, outside balls hit back in your stance and inside balls hit forward in your stance. You also may notice that outside pitches are not as outside as you had previously thought, due to your improved, tighter swing. You may have to move your stance closer to the plate than you have been.
- The "zero" is sometimes the hardest in the beginning because you are learning to use both your forward momentum *and* your front knee to supply the power to your swing. In time, it becomes comfortable.
- If you are having trouble with the "ones" and "twos," try focusing on keeping your back leg rigid through the stride. I find that players who have trouble with "ones" and "twos" are often trying to rush into the Cushion by bending their back leg too much prior to falling forward in the stride. You can't rush gravity. Let yourself fall forward naturally, allowing gravity to work in its own time.

HELPFUL PRACTICE TIPS

Setting up Stations. For individuals or teams, the above drills work well in stations. If you have video available, make the Zero One Two Drill the video station.

Quality over quantity. Positional Training requires concentration and focus on your positions. Pace yourself through the training and concentrate fully on your mechanics rather than trying to swing as many times as possible. Just because you are breathing heavy and getting tired does not mean you are getting better. If you need to stretch, get a drink, or just take a break, do it. Remember that in games, the ball doesn't care how "hard you worked" when you make contact. All that matters when you make contact are the positions you achieved through the swing.

CONCLUSION

THE ART OF POSITIONAL HITTING

"The most incomprehensible thing about the world is that it is comprehensible."
— Albert Einstein

By now, I hope you understand that the best opportunity to make significant and rapid improvement to your hitting is through positional change. Properly analyzing your swing on video after games will provide you with the accurate feedback around which you can design your training program.

When you begin to hit poorly, don't just hope that your swing will come around again. Look at your swing positions on video; find out precisely what is going wrong and fix it. Always fall back on your technique. Video, not feel, should be your only master.

I recently worked with a player who had an article written about him in the local paper about how well he had been hitting, and the pressure to perform started to get to him. He became over-cautious at the plate and it affected his positions through the swing. I told him that there was an easy remedy: fall back on your technique. "When that article came out," I told him, "it was certainly a reason to be proud. After your initial excitement, however, realize that nothing should distract you from your analysis and training. The main problem is not in your head, it's just that something has distracted you from your regular positional analysis and training. You have done great in making improvements in your positions but you have a long way to go. That article simply made you lose sight of that. Get to work on improving your swing."

Positional Hitting is a philosophy as much as it is a technique. Distractions will come in many different forms and, if you are not aware of them, can sway your focus from your swing mechanics. It's important that you recognize these distractions and never let them pull you away from the endless pursuit of better swing positions.

FEEL IS NOT REAL

I often receive calls from players who want to talk about their swing over the phone. They will say something like: "I feel like my hands are coming out of the zone" or "I'm falling off of the ball." I actually don't know what these phrases mean (and I don't want to know) but I do hear them from time to time. I'll stop them before we begin talking about mechanics and tell them, "Feel is not real. If you can't talk to me in terms of the positions and angles you are seeing, then go back and analyze your swing on video and call me back."

I'm not trying to be difficult when I tell them this; it is just so important that players get out of the habit of quickly diagnosing their swing faults by using vague phrases that don't get to the heart of the problem. Be patient and take your time when analyzing where your swing is going wrong. The only accurate and reliable source of feedback comes from the feedback attained from your video analysis.

TRAIN AS IF

It's OK to doubt. It's natural. In some cases, it keeps you motivated. The only time that there can be no doubt in your mind at all is when you are training. You must train as if you fully expect to accomplish all of your hitting goals. Your confidence and belief will develop naturally, provided you do the proper training. Most people will not do the work that is necessary to succeed because they think of reasons why they shouldn't work instead of thinking of reasons why they should.

Really, that's the only true battle that exists. Defeat the voice in your mind that says, "I'll skip today. I can just train tomorrow." If you can convince that voice to do the work today, even if only for a few minutes, then you've won the real battle.

ODDSITIVE VS. POSITIVE MENTALITY

I prefer an Oddsitive mentality over a positive mentality. An Oddsitive mentality is one in which you understand that every at-bat has odds of success and failure attached to it. With an Oddsitive mentality, you understand that you can never completely control the outcome, but you can stack the odds in your favor. Many factors come into play, including the positions you've trained, the pitchers ability, and plain luck. The fact is, sometimes you will fail and sometimes you will succeed. The only thing you can control is improving the odds, to stack them in your favor as much as possible prior to every pitch.

The player with an Oddsitive mentality will smoothly ride the inherent ups and downs associated with the sport of hitting. He will therefore have far more potential for success than a player with a positive mentality. The bottom line is that you are occasionally going to fail. If you never failed, the game wouldn't be a challenge and wouldn't be worth pursuing. Your mindset should not be one that puts undue pressure on you by ignoring your poor performances, as is the case in a positive mental approach. Your mentality should be that you will continuously work to increase your odds of success, and on game day, let the chips fall where they may. It's a continuous pursuit, turning both good and bad games into valuable learning opportunities.

An Oddsitive mentality is one in which you are not afraid of the most negative possible outcome. To practice the Oddsitive mentality, before games visualize the worst possible outcome and handling it with class and confidence before visualizing the positive outcomes that you desire.

On game-day, let go and play. Provided that you film your game at-bats, you can learn from your mistakes and failures after the game. Any "trying hard" on game-day is pointless. The hard work should have already been done.

Athletes have been conditioned to try to avoid negative thoughts. That approach only makes them worse. Don't fight the thoughts that come to your mind. Instead, welcome them. They may be trying to teach you something; they may also be worthless. Listen to them and then decide if they can help you in any way. Never push a thought away. If you try to avoid a negative thought, like ignoring a child, it will only get louder.

The goal is to be able to perform well regardless of what pops into your head. That is done through your training, through repetition. I played with a middle infielder who would make the most spectacular plays in the field. He was known on the team for his extra practice. He would work on all types of flashy plays after practice by having players hit him grounders far to his left and right. One day, I asked him about his mentality after he made three outstanding plays in a tight and intense game. He said, "I had a great song playing in my mind." That's when it really hit me: the quality of your practice, the attention to proper form, is what gives you the ability to perform well when others would most likely choke.

If you do the adequate amount of quality repetitions away from the game, then you won't have to force any positive thoughts at all during competition. Your body will react automatically. All you have to do is let go and free your mind (and maybe leave some room for your favorite song).

After games, the player with an Oddsitive mentality is unafraid to look at his faults. In fact, he is more interested in what he did wrong than what he did right. Again, video will be the key to attaining accurate feedback.

SWING ADVICE FOR THE GREATS

The swing is an ever evolving art. If we are to let the swing evolve, we have to search for areas within the positions where improvements can be made. And there is no better opportunity to let the swing evolve than to critique the swings of the greatest players ever. By doing so, you begin to understand the swing of the future. The following is swing advice that I would have given to a few of the greatest hitters in history.

BABE RUTH

Babe Ruth, overall, had the best swing positions I've ever measured. His Slot and Impact positions were outstanding. His Cushion, however, placed him in position to be fooled on off-speed pitches. Specifically, his Angle S was low, about 16 degrees. Translated, this means that when his front heel hit in his stride, he had already begun opening his shoulders, committing to the pitch earlier than necessary. The Zero One Two Drill would have been great for Ruth.

TED WILLIAMS

Ted Williams had one of the best Impact positions ever and achieved solid Cushion and Fall positions as well. However, Williams could have added more power to his swing by improving his Angle L in the Slot. The Slot Drill, with a focus on feeling the bat whip behind him toward the pitcher as he opened up to swing, would have been a great drill for Williams.

PETE ROSE

Pete Rose had a very quick swing, which helped him achieve the most base hits in history. At the time he played, the prevailing wisdom was that small guys should be "slap" hitters and he played that role to a tee. However, with his quickness and athleticism, it would have been interesting to see how many home runs he would have hit with a better Impact position. Rose's CSR averaged between 310 and 330.

Rose had a lightning fast body rotation. Unfortunately, his back arm extension was just as fast. Working on the IB Drill and quieting his back arm extension, letting the speed of his body rotation control the move and whip the bat into the hitting zone, would have helped Rose achieve more power without sacrificing his legendary consistency. Instead of 160 career home runs, he may have had 460.

LABELS

Labels belong on canned foods, not on people. If your parents, coaches, or peers label you as a certain type of hitter, it is important to understand that you can hit with *both* power and consistency. The limits that you place on yourself are ultimately controlled by you. Here are some ways to combat the labels that others try to place on you.

Express your goals openly to others. Expressing your goals openly proves that you are serious about your goals and starts to chip away at the labels that you have previously placed on yourself.

Expect doubters. If you are wondering whether or not others are going to doubt you, I'll put your worries to rest: they will. That goes for your family and friends too. But the good news is that this can be a source of motivation. The great basketball player, Michael Jordan, loved doubters because he enjoyed - truly enjoyed - proving them wrong.

Labels are often wrong anyway. It's always interesting to look back on the first week of practice after a season and think about what players were projected to be the most valuable on the team by the coach, the newspapers, etc. By season's end, it is often a different set of guys who were the stars of the team.

Dear Positional Hitter:

My goal for this book is to allow players to experience the feeling of hitting like you've always wanted. Please send your comments, questions, or stories to me: jaime@ theswingmechanic.com.

Enjoy your never ending pursuit of a more perfect swing!
Jaime Cevallos (The Swing Mechanic)

For the latest in Positional Hitting, go to **www.positionalhitting.com**

CPSIA information can be obtained at www.ICGtesting.com
259760BV00007B/11/P